Betty Crocker
decorating
cakes and cupcakes

WILEY

Wiley Publishing, Inc.

Library of Congress Cataloging-in-Publication Data

Betty Crocker decorating cakes and cupcakes / Betty Crocker editors.
    p. cm.
  Includes index.
  ISBN-13 978-0-471-75307-0 (pbk.)
  ISBN-10 0-471-75307-6 (pbk.)
  1. Cake decorating. 2. Cake. I. Crocker, Betty.
  TX771.2.B47 2006
  641.8'6539–dc22   2005032314

Manufactured in the United States of America

10 9 8 7 6 5 4 3 2 1

Cover photo: Purse Cake (page 47), Happy Birthday Marshmallow Cupcakes (page 118) and Bug Cupcakes (page 128)

GENERAL MILLS

Director, Book and Online Publishing: Kim Walter

Manager, Cookbook Publishing: Lois Tlusty

Editor: Cheri Olerud

Recipe Development and Testing: Betty Crocker Kitchens

Photography and Food Styling: General Mills Photography Studios

WILEY PUBLISHING, INC.

Publisher: Natalie Chapman

Executive Editor: Anne Ficklen

Editor: Kristi Hart

Production Editor: Ava Wilder

Cover Design: Suzanne Sunwoo

Interior Design and Layout: Holly Wittenberg

Color Lab: Clint Lahnen

Photography Art Direction: Janet Skalicky

Manufacturing Manager: Kevin Watt

The Betty Crocker Kitchens seal guarantees success in your kitchen. Every recipe has been tested in America's Most Trusted Kitchens™ to meet our high standards of reliability, easy preparation and great taste.

FIND MORE GREAT IDEAS AND SHOP FOR NAME-BRAND HOUSEWARES AT

BettyCrocker.com

Dear Friends,

Ready to create some magic, right in your own kitchen? Baking and decorating a homemade birthday cake or cupcakes is a wonderful, magical memory, a warm tradition that never loses its childhood charm. And what adult doesn't love to be remembered with a home-baked cake?

Whatever the occasion, everything you need to decorate beautiful cakes and whimsical cupcakes is included in *Betty Crocker Decorating Cakes and Cupcakes*. There are fabulously fun, absolutely adorable ideas to turn your cakes and cupcakes into works of art. And the simple-to-follow recipes and instructions will have you easily putting the pieces together.

Try the adorable Purse Cake (page 47) for the little girl in your life, the Happy Birthday Marshmallow Cupcakes (page 118) for an office birthday, or the Bug Cupcakes (page 128) for your next outdoor picnic. Let these unforgettable, home-baked treats really take the cake at your next get-together.

Baking and decorating—it's fun stuff to do together.

Warmly,

Betty Crocker

Contents

Cake Walk

The Basics

Baking and decorating cakes for a special occasion is so rewarding! Watching others' eyes light up when they see your creation makes it all worthwhile. For the easiest baking, frosting and decorating of your clever cakes, follow the steps below. With a little practice, you'll gain the extra confidence you need to get great results every time.

Many of the recipes in this cookbook are for scratch cakes. Cake mixes can successfully be substituted in recipes calling for scratch cakes; each recipe tells you how. Even more convenient, many of the recipes in this cookbook call for cake mix.

Cupcakes, lovely little bites of cake that everyone loves and are incredibly easy to bake and fun to decorate, are also found throughout the book.

Getting Started

If you're familiar with baking, you know that baking is both a science and an art. As in science, it's important to be accurate—while measuring, mixing and baking. As in art, you can use your creativity to individualize your cake.

Measuring

DRY INGREDIENTS

1. Use graduated nested measuring cups to measure nonliquids.

2. For granulated sugar, dip the cup into the sugar to fill, then level with a straight-edged knife or spatula.

3. To measure flour or powdered sugar, lightly spoon into cup, then level with a straight-edged knife or spatula. (Sift powdered sugar before measuring only if lumpy.)

4. To measure brown sugar and shortening, measure by pressing firmly into cup with a spoon or rubber spatula, then leveling off excess with a straight-edged knife or spatula.

5. For nuts, coconut and cut-up fruits, lightly spoon into cup, then pack lightly.

   To measure butter or margarine, follow the markings on paper or foil wrapper showing tablespoon and cup amounts; use a sharp knife to cut off the amount you need. Or measure by pressing firmly into cup with a spoon or rubber spatula, then leveling off excess with a straight-edged knife or spatula.

LIQUID INGREDIENTS

Use glass measuring cups to measure oil, water and milk. Bend down and read the measurement at eye level, or use an angled measuring cup.

MEASURING SPOONS

1. Use graduated measuring spoons to measure dry ingredients and small amounts of thin and thick liquids. If you do not have a 1/8 teaspoon measuring spoon, fill a 1/4 teaspoon measuring spoon and remove half.

2. Pour thin liquids into spoon until full.

3. For thick liquids like honey or syrup, pour into spoon until full, then level with a straight-edged knife or spatula.

Beating Cake Batter

You can use either a portable or a standard electric mixer. Because standard mixers are more powerful than portable, reduce the speed to low during the first step of beating the ingredients to prevent spattering.

You can also mix cakes by hand. Stir the ingredients to moisten and blend, then beat 150 strokes for every minute of beating time (3 minutes equals 450 strokes).

Using Eggs

The cake recipes use large eggs. Eggs can also be purchased in medium and extra-large sizes. If using medium or extra-large, refer to the Egg Volumes chart below for the correct equivalent.

EGG VOLUMES

Large Eggs	Measurement
2 eggs	1/3 to 1/2 cup
3 eggs	1/2 to 2/3 cup
4 eggs	2/3 to 1 cup
1 egg white	about 2 tablespoons
1 egg yolk	about 1 1/2 tablespoons

For the greatest volume, let egg whites stand at room temperature about 15 minutes before beating. Beat whites in a clean, dry metal bowl with a clean beater. Any bit of yolk or fat in the whites will prevent them from beating properly.

Leftover egg whites can be stored covered in the refrigerator 7 to 10 days. To freeze whites, place in a plastic ice-cube tray, then remove the frozen cubes to a plastic freezer bag for storage. Thaw frozen whites in the refrigerator.

Leftover egg yolks can be covered with a bit of water and stored in a covered container in the refrigerator 2 to 3 days. Leftover yolks can be used in custards, scrambled eggs, boiled dressings, egg pastries and cake fillings.

Selecting Pans

For the best baked cakes:

- Use the size of pan called for in the recipe. To check the pan width, measure across the top from inside edge to inside edge. Baking a cake in too large a pan results in a pale, flat, shrunken cake. If the pan is too small or too shallow, the cake will bulge and lose its shape.

- Use shiny metal pans, if you have them, as the best choice for cakes. They reflect heat away from the cake and produce a tender, light brown crust. If you are using dark or nonstick pans or glass baking dishes, follow the manufacturer's directions. These pans readily absorb heat, so reduce the baking temperature by 25°F.

- Fill cake pans no more than half full. If you are using a pan with an unusual shape (heart, star, bell), measure the capacity by filling with water, measuring the water and using half that amount of batter. (Cupcakes can be made from remaining batter.)

- Place oven racks in the middle of the oven and place pans in the center of the rack. Do not let layer pans touch, and allow at least one inch of space between the pans and the oven sides.

- Use silicone pans, the newest in bakeware, as another good choice; they're recommended by the Betty Crocker Kitchens for baking cakes and cupcakes. Cakes baked in them brown evenly. Because silicone pans are so flexible, place them on a cookie sheet before adding cake batter. Use the cookie sheet to remove the pan from oven.

CAKE YIELDS

Size and Type of Cake	Number of Servings
8-inch layer	10 to 14
9-inch layer	12 to 16
9-inch loaf	8 to 10
8- or 9-inch square	9
13 × 9–inch rectangle	12 to 15
10-inch angel food (tube)	12 to 16
12-cup fluted tube	12 to 16

Removing Cakes from Pans

Cool cake in pans on wire racks for ten minutes. Cover one rack with a towel; place towel side down on top of cake; turn over as a unit and remove pan.

Place a rack on bottom of cake; turn over both racks so the cake is right side up. Remove towel. Allow cakes to cool completely on racks, about one hour.

Splitting Cake Layers

TOOTHPICK GUIDES: Using toothpicks, mark middle points on sides of cake. Using picks as a guide, cut through the cake with long, thin sharp knife.

THREAD TRICK: Split cake by pulling a piece of heavy sewing thread horizontally, back and forth, through the cake.

Backgrounds for Cut-Up Cakes

Cakes may be placed on trays, large cutting boards or upside-down 15 × 10 × 1–inch pans. If you do not have a tray large enough:

- Cut a piece of cardboard two to four inches larger than the assembled cake. Cover the background with regular or colored foil, colored plastic wrap or freezer paper. To vary the color or fit the occasion, you can use shelf paper, gift wrap, colored tissue paper or a home-drawn creation, then cover with clear cellophane or plastic wrap.

- Messages or other designs can be added to the background around the cake with either a marking pencil or piped frosting.

To Frost or Not to Frost

If you choose not to frost your cake or cupcakes, you can glaze or dust; here's how:

- **GLAZE.** Choose one of the glaze recipes, page 150. Evenly spread or drizzle in interesting design over top of cooled cake or cupcakes. For ease, pour glaze into a heavy food-storage plastic bag, snip off a tiny corner of the bag and squeeze. If you want a thicker drizzle, snip off a slightly larger corner.

- **DUST.** Powdered sugar dusts a cake nicely. Dust lightly or as desired through a shaker, sieve or sifter. For a more dramatic look, place a doily, stencil or simple cutout shape on the cake before dusting, then carefully remove the pattern.

Making Frosting

For foolproof frosting that spreads easily:

- Sift powdered sugar to be used for a decorating frosting to make it completely free of lumps (even small lumps must be sifted to avoid grainy frosting).

- Make the frosting the right consistency. To add borders and drop flowers, a medium consistency frosting works best. Roses and other flowers need a firmer frosting so the petals will hold their shape. Frosting can be slightly thinner for writing and for making leaves and simple line designs.

Frosting Cut-Up Cakes

Freeze whole cakes and cut-up cakes (place cut pieces of cake on a cookie sheet) for about an hour before frosting to minimize crumbling. To "crumb-coat" exposed cut edges before frosting to help control crumbling, mix water, a teaspoon at a time, into a small amount of frosting to make a thin frosting, then spread a smooth, thin layer onto cut surfaces and freeze.

Keep frostings covered with plastic wrap while working to prevent them from drying out.

Frosting Layer Cakes

1. Place four strips of waxed paper around the edge of cake plate. Brush away any loose crumbs from the cooled cake layer. Place the layer on the plate, rounded side down. (The waxed paper will protect the plate as you frost and can be removed later.)

2. Spread about 1/3 cup creamy frosting (1/2 cup fluffy frosting) over the top of the first layer to within about 1/4 inch of edge.

3. Place the second layer, rounded side up, on the first layer so that the flat sides of the layers are together with frosting in between. Coat the side of the cake with a very thin layer of frosting to seal in the crumbs.

4. Frost the side of the cake in swirls, making a rim about 1/4 inch high above the top of the cake to prevent the top from appearing sloped. Spread remaining frosting on top, just to the built-up rim.

Cutting Frosted Cakes

Follow these easy steps when cutting cakes:

- Use a sharp, thin knife to cut shortening-type cakes and a long serrated knife for angel food cakes.

- If the frosting sticks, dip the knife in hot water and wipe with a damp paper towel after cutting each slice.

- Cover exposed cut ends with plastic wrap to maintain moistness.

- To learn how to cut wedding cakes, see page 91.

Freezing Cakes

Unfrosted cakes and cupcakes freeze better than frosted cakes. When freezing unfrosted cakes:

- Cool cakes completely, at least one hour.

- Place cakes in cardboard bakery boxes to prevent crushing, then cover with foil, plastic wrap or large freezer bags. Properly packaged, unfrosted cakes can be kept frozen three to four months.

- Freeze cakes in single pieces or smaller portions to thaw quickly.

For frosted cakes, creamy-type frostings freeze best. Fluffy-type and whipped cream frostings freeze well but may stick to the wrapping. To prevent frosting from sticking, freeze cake uncovered 1 hour, then insert toothpicks around the top and side of cake, and wrap. Frozen frosted cakes keep two to three months.

Decorating gel, hard candies and colored sugars do not freeze well because they tend to run during thawing.

Storing Unfrosted and Frosted Cakes

To keep your baked cakes fresh:

- Cool cakes completely, at least one hour, before storing. If covered when warm, they become sticky and difficult to frost.

- Cover cakes that will be frosted later loosely so the surface stays dry. If covered tightly, they become sticky and difficult to frost.

- Store cakes with a creamy-type frosting under a cake safe (or large inverted bowl), or cover loosely with foil, plastic wrap or waxed paper.

- Store cakes with whipped cream toppings or cream fillings in the refrigerator.

- Frost a cake with fluffy frosting on the day it is to be served. Fluffy frostings are not as stable as creamy frostings because of the air incorporated into them. If you must store the cake overnight, place it under a cake safe or inverted bowl and slip a wooden spoon handle or a knife blade under the rim so the cover is not airtight.

Getting Ready to Decorate

Before decorating, assemble everything you need.

- Use a turntable or lazy Susan to make decorating easier and faster. Keep turning as you use different decorating items.

- When adding food color, frosting will darken slightly as it sets. For vivid or deeper food colors, use paste or gel food color.

DECORATING BAGS

Cake decorating bags include reusable plastic-coated decorating bags and disposable parchment paper or plastic bags. The plastic-coated decorating bag can be used with or without a coupler. The coupler allows you to change decorating tips while still using the same bag of frosting. A coupler is not used for large decorating tips.

Fitting Your New Decorating Bag with a Coupler

1. Unscrew the ring from the coupler base and drop the base, narrow end first, down into the end of the bag. Push the coupler base as far down into the bag as possible.

2. With a pencil, mark the location of the coupler's bottom thread on the outside of the bag. Push the coupler up and out of the bag.

3. Cut off the end of the decorating bag at the pencil mark. (Be careful not to cut too much; you can always trim a little more later if necessary.)

4. Replace the coupler base in the bag, pushing it down so the two bottom threads of the coupler show through the open end of the bag. Place decorating tip in ring and screw onto coupler base.

Now for the fun part! Remember these tips as you decorate.

- Lightly outline the design with a toothpick to use as a guide before piping a design or a message on a cake. Short strips of sewing thread can be lightly placed on the frosted cake to mark the position of the message.

- Most designs are made by holding the decorating bag at a 45° angle.

- For drop flowers, stars, dots and rosettes, hold the bag at a 90° angle (perpendicular to the surface).

- Use steady pressure to press out the frosting as you work. The amount of pressure will determine the size and evenness of any design. To finish a design, stop the pressure and lift the point up and away.

How to Use Your Decorating Bag

1. If not using a coupler or if the decorating tip is large, simply place the tip in the bag. If using a coupler, place the desired decorating tip on the coupler base and screw the coupler ring into place over the tip to hold it securely. With tip in place, you're ready to fill the bag with frosting.

2. To fill the bag with frosting or whipped cream, fold down the open end of the bag to form a cuff approximately two inches wide. Hold the bag beneath the cuff and, using a spatula, fill the bag half full with frosting. (Don't fill the bag too full or frosting will back up out of the bag.)

3. To close the bag, unfold the cuff and twist the top of the bag, forcing the frosting down into the tip. Continue to twist end of bag as you decorate.

4. To change decorating tips, unscrew the coupler ring, remove the tip, replace it with another tip and screw the ring on again.

HOW TO USE DECORATING TIPS

Practice on paper first to get comfortable using the decorating bag and tips.

DROP FLOWER: Popular drop flower tips include numbers 107, 129, 190, 217, 224, 225, 1C and 2D. These tips are the easiest for a beginning cake decorator to make flowers with because they are made directly on the frosted cake. The number of petals is determined by the number of openings in the end of the tip. Drop flower tips can be used to make either plain or swirled drop flowers.

LEAF: Popular leaf tips include 65, 67 and 352. The V-shaped opening of this tip forms the pointed end of the leaf. Leaf tips make plain, ruffled or stand-up leaves. Leaf tips can also be used to make attractive borders.

PETAL: Tip numbers 101, 102, 103 and 104 are used for making roses, wild roses, violets, sweet peas and carnations. They are also used for making ribbons, bows, swags and ruffles. For very large roses, number 127 can be used.

STAR: Popular star tips include numbers 13 through 22 and range in size from small to very large. Large star tips include numbers 32, 43 and 8B.

These tips are used for making shell, rope and zigzag borders, stars and rosettes, and they can also be used for making drop flowers.

WRITING: Popular writing tips include numbers 1 through 4 (small), 12 (medium) and 1A and 2A (large). Writing tips are also called plain or round tips. These tips can also be used to make beads, dots, balls, stems, vines and flower centers.

How to Make:

ROSETTES: Using a star tip, squeeze out whipped cream or frosting into a circle, using steady, even pressure. Then without stopping, swirl the whipped cream on top in a similar circle, finally ending the swirl in a peak as you decrease the pressure.

SIMPLE DESIGNS: Using a writing tip, hold the decorating bag at a 45° angle. With the tip raised slightly from the surface, squeeze the bag, applying pressure evenly, and direct the tip to outline the desired design. To end the design, stop squeezing, touch tip to surface and pull away.

BORDERS: Make each border by holding the decorating bag at a 45° angle to the surface.

SHELL: This is a series of shells connected in a continuous line. Using a star tip, squeeze out frosting using consistent heavy pressure to create a full base. Raise the tip as shell builds up. Decrease pressure, drawing frosting to a point. Begin the next shell directly over that point.

REVERSE SHELL: This border is similar to the plain shell border except that as the shell is built up, circle to the right and decrease pressure. The second shell is circled to the left. Continue, alternating shells from right to left.

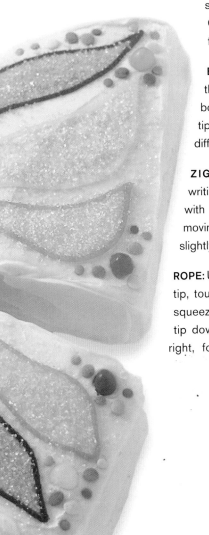

BEAD: This technique is the same as the shell border except uses a writing tip. Vary pressure to make different sizes of beads.

ZIGZAG: Using a star or writing tip, squeeze out frosting with a steady, even pressure, moving bag from side to side slightly to form a zigzag line.

ROPE: Using a star or large writing tip, touch tip to the surface and squeeze the bag, moving the tip down, up and around to the right, forming a slight S curve.

Stop pressure and pull the tip away. Place the tip under bottom curve of the first S and repeat the procedure. Continue joining S curves to form rope.

SWAG: Using a star, petal or writing tip, as you squeeze out frosting, move the tip down and up, down and up, as if writing a continuous letter S. Use steady, even pressure as you repeat the procedure. When completed, discontinue pressure and pull the tip away.

NO DECORATING BAG?

If you don't have a decorating bag, you can make a cone from a food-storage plastic bag or paper envelope. Place 1/2 cup frosting in the corner of the bag and seal, or place 1/3 cup frosting in the corner of an envelope and fold the sides of the envelope toward the center. Snip a small piece off the corner to make a tip.

NEW AND EASY WAYS TO DECORATE

After frosting, add a special touch to create a new look.

PEARL SUGAR: White sugar grains add interest to cakes and cupcakes for special occasions like showers and weddings.

CRYSTAL AND SANDING SUGAR: Sprinkle this glistening, colorful sugar on frosted cakes and cupcakes.

FOOD WRITER PENS: Use as you would ink markers to add dazzling color.

DECORATING SPRAY: Spray on cakes and cupcakes; it dries to form a powdery coating. The look is similar to a technique used by bakeries.

Chocolate Basics

Nothing is comparable to the look of chocolate for your lovely decorated cakes. And who doesn't love the indulgent flavor of chocolate? You can melt chocolate easily on the stove-top or in the microwave. Chocolate chips can be melted as they are; it's best to break or chop bars of baking chocolate into smaller pieces before melting. Follow one of these three easy ways to melt chocolate:

- Heat chocolate in a heavy saucepan over low heat, stirring occasionally, until almost melted. Remove from heat and stir until completely melted.

- Place ½ to 1 cup chocolate chips or 1 to 3 ounces of baking chocolate in small micro-wavable bowl. Microwave uncovered on Medium (50%) for two to three minutes for chocolate chips or 1½ to 2½ minutes for baking chocolate, stirring after half the time, until softened. Stir until smooth.

- Place chocolate in a small, heatproof bowl placed in hot water or in the top of a double boiler over hot (not boiling) water, and stir occasionally until melted.

Chocolate Cure

"Seizing" occurs when a very small amount of water or moisture causes chocolate to become thick, lumpy and grainy during melting. To avoid seizing, be sure all utensils are completely dry and that no moisture gets into the chocolate while it melts. If it happens, cure the problem by stirring in about 1 teaspoon shortening for each ounce of chocolate being melted to return chocolate to a creamy consistency.

STORING CHOCOLATE

To maintain good quality, store chocolate in a cool, dry place between 60° and 78°F. If the temperature is higher than 78°F or the humidity is above 50 percent, keep chocolate wrapped in moistureproof wrap. Store chocolate in the refrigerator tightly wrapped to keep out moisture and odors. Remove it from the refrigerator and let stand at room temp-erature for a few minutes before using.

Chocolate Designs

You can use chocolate in many ways to make your cakes look special.

CHOCOLATE CURLS: The curls will be easier to make if the chocolate is at room temperature. Place a bar or block of chocolate on waxed paper. Make curls by pulling a vegetable peeler toward you in long, thin strokes while pressing firmly against the chocolate. (If curls crumble or stay too straight, chocolate may be too cold. Placing heel of hand on chocolate will warm it enough to get good curls.) Transfer each curl carefully with a toothpick to a waxed paper–lined cookie sheet or directly onto frosted cake.

CHOCOLATE CUTOUTS: Melt 4 ounces of sweet cooking chocolate or semisweet baking chocolate. Spread over outside bottom of 8-inch square pan. Refrigerate until firm; bring to room temperature. Use cookie cutters in desired shapes and sizes to make cutouts. Refrigerate until ready to place on cake or dessert. Make cutouts extra special by dipping half of each cutout in melted white chocolate and refrigerating again until set.

CHOCOLATE TWIGS: Melt 2 ounces of white chocolate baking bar or semisweet baking chocolate and 1 teaspoon shortening. Pour into decorating bag with small writing tip. Squeeze melted chocolate onto waxed paper into twig shapes; sprinkle with white decorator sugar crystals if desired. Let dry. Peel twigs from waxed paper; arrange on cake.

CHOCOLATE LEAVES: Wash and dry 12 to 18 fresh unsprayed leaves (lemon, grape or rose) or pliable plastic leaves. Melt 2 ounces white chocolate baking bar, 1/2 cup (3 oz) semisweet chocolate chips or 2 squares (1 oz each) semisweet chocolate and 1 teaspoon shortening. Brush chocolate about 1/8 inch thick over backs of leaves using small brush. Refrigerate until firm, at least 1 hour. Peel off leaves, handling as little as possible; refrigerate until ready to use.

CHOCOLATE RIBBONS: Melt 4 ounces of white chocolate baking bar or semisweet baking chocolate. Spread with a metal spatula in a thin layer on a large cookie sheet. Refrigerate about 10 minutes or just until chocolate is firm. (Do not refrigerate until hard or chocolate will break. If chocolate gets too hard, let stand at room temperature.) Scrape strips of chocolate with a knife or metal pastry scraper. Hold the knife flat to the sheet and pull slowly and carefully toward you, curling ribbons as you go. (See photo of Apricot-Almond Wedding Cake, page 92.)

SHAVED CHOCOLATE: All types of chocolate can be used to make shaved chocolate. Pull a vegetable peeler across the surface of a bar or block of chocolate, using short, quick strokes. Or use a vegetable shredder with large holes. Sprinkle on frosted cake.

CHOCOLATE DRIZZLES: After melting chocolate, pour into resealable food-storage plastic bag, press down into corner of bag, snip off a small corner of bag and drizzle melted chocolate over surface.

For more information, go to:

BettyCrocker.com

Cut-Out and Shaped Cakes

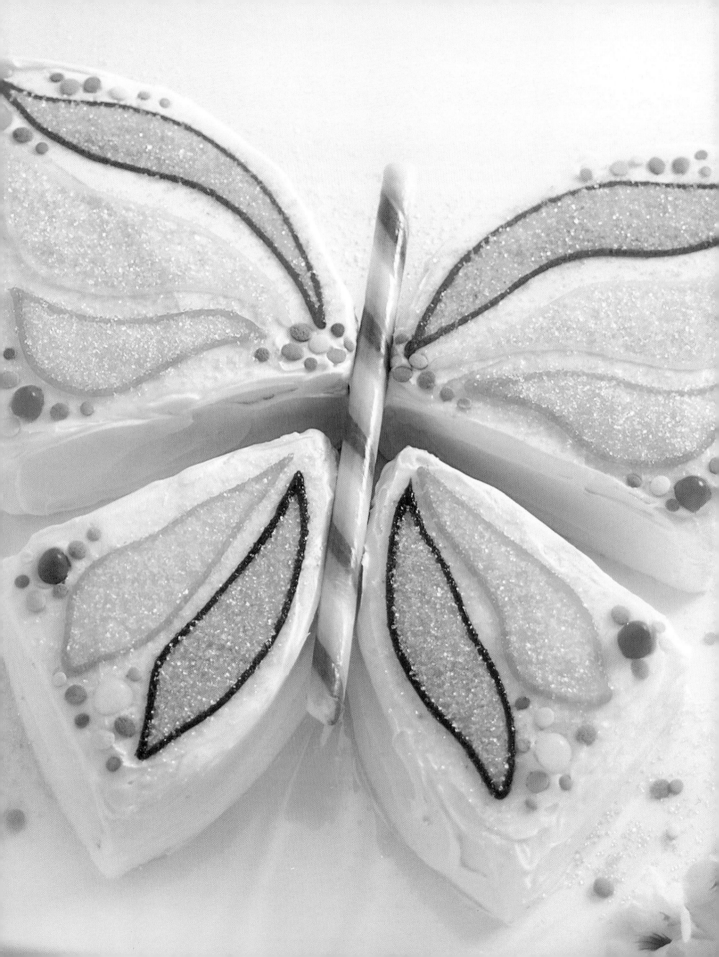

Little Deuce Coupe Cakes

1 box (1 lb 2.25 oz) yellow cake mix with pudding

Water, oil and eggs called for on cake mix box

2 containers (1 lb each) vanilla creamy frosting

Blue, red, green and yellow liquid food colors

Tray or cardboard, 20 × 16 inches, covered

Red or black string licorice

8 yellow round starlight candies

10 creme-filled chocolate sandwich cookies

1 red or orange gumdrop

2 birthday cake candles

1. Heat oven to 350°F. Grease bottoms only of three 8 × 4–inch loaf pans with shortening or cooking spray. Make cake mix as directed on box, using water, oil and eggs. Divide batter evenly among pans.

2. Bake 28 to 33 minutes or until toothpick inserted in center comes out clean. Cool 10 minutes. Run knife around sides of pans to loosen cakes; remove from pans to wire rack. Cool completely, about 1 hour. Freeze cakes uncovered about 1 hour for easier frosting if desired.

3. Remove ¼ cup frosting from each container; set aside. To make purple frosting, stir 8 drops blue food color and 8 drops red food color into 1 container of frosting. To make green frosting, stir 3 drops green food color and 3 drops yellow food color into other container of frosting.

4. On tray, place 2 loaves, rounded sides down; frost one with about two-thirds of the purple frosting; frost the other with two-thirds of the green frosting. Cut remaining loaf crosswise in half; taper the cut edges slightly to form windshields. Place one half on each cake for cab, placing about 3 inches from front edge and with tapered windshield side toward front of car. Frost windows of cabs with reserved vanilla frosting; frost top and edges with colored frosting. Use licorice to outline windows and make bumpers. Add starlight candies for headlights and taillights; add cookies for wheels and the spares. Place gumdrop on top of 1 car for beacon and add candles for radio antennae.

1 Serving (Cake and Frosting): Calories 460 (Calories from Fat 200); Total Fat 22g (Saturated Fat 7g; Trans Fat 5g); Cholesterol 40mg; Sodium 380mg; Total Carbohydrates 63g (Dietary Fiber 0g; Sugars 49g) • **% Daily Value:** Vitamin A 0%; Vitamin C 0%; Calcium 6%; Iron 4% • **Exchanges:** 1 Starch, 3 Other Carbohydrates, 4½ Fat • **Carbohydrate Choices:** 4

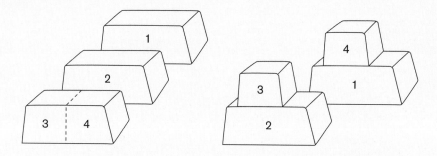

Rabbit Cake

Carrot Cake (page 138)

Creamy White Frosting (page 147)

Tray or cardboard, 20 × 16 inches, covered

Colored sugar

Black shoestring licorice

2 white or pink marshmallow-covered chocolate cake balls with creamy filling

2 large black gumdrops

1 pink licorice candy

1 large red gumdrop

2 pieces candy-coated gum

2 sticks striped fruit-flavored gum

1. Bake Carrot Cake as directed for two 8- or 9-inch rounds. Cut one round as shown in diagram. Freeze pieces uncovered about 1 hour for easier frosting if desired. Make Creamy White Frosting. On tray, arrange pieces as shown in diagram. Frost head and ears with white frosting, attaching pieces with small amount of frosting. Frost bow tie; sprinkle with colored sugar and outline with shoestring licorice.

2. Arrange cake balls on frosting for cheeks. Insert short strips of shoestring licorice into cheeks for whiskers. Outline eyes with shoestring licorice; add short strips for eyelashes. Use black gumdrops for pupils of eyes, pink licorice candy for nose, red gumdrop for mouth and candy-coated gum for teeth. Cut striped gum into long oval pieces and place in center of ears. Decorate with magician hat and magic wand if desired.

1 Serving (Cake and Frosting): Calories 360 (Calories from Fat 190); Total Fat 21g (Saturated Fat 3g; Trans Fat 0g); Cholesterol 40mg; Sodium 180mg; Total Carbohydrates 37g (Dietary Fiber 2g; Sugars 22g) • **% Daily Value:** Vitamin A 80%; Vitamin C 0%; Calcium 2%; Iron 8% • **Exchanges:** 1 Starch, 1 1/2 Other Carbohydrates, 4 Fat • **Carbohydrate Choices:** 2 1/2

Time-Saver Tip: Substitute 1 box (1 lb 2 oz) carrot cake mix or 1 box (1 lb 2.25 oz) yellow cake mix with pudding for the Carrot Cake. Bake as directed for two 8- or 9-inch rounds. Substitute 2 containers (1 lb each) creamy white frosting for the Creamy White Frosting.

Ballet Slippers Cake

1. Bake White Cake as directed for 13 × 9–inch rectangle. Cut cake as shown in diagram. Freeze pieces uncovered about 1 hour for easier frosting if desired. Make Creamy White Frosting; reserve 1 cup. Tint remaining frosting with 3 drops food color; reserve 1/2 cup.

2. On tray, arrange cake pieces. Trim pieces to form slippers. Frost sides of both slippers with pink frosting. Frost top of each slipper about 3 inches from the edge for the toes, tapering to about 1 inch around the outside edge for the rest of the slipper. Frost the center oval with reserved white frosting. Let frosting set a few minutes. To give frosting a fabric-like appearance, carefully cover frosting with a paper towel and gently pat; remove towel.

3. Place reserved 1/2 cup pink frosting in decorating bag fitted with writing tip #5. Pipe a small beaded border where pink frosting edge meets white edge. Pipe a small bow at each toe with pink or white frosting. For laces, attach ribbon to slippers.

White Cake (page 143)
Creamy White Frosting (page 147)
Red liquid food color
Tray or cardboard, 20 × 15 inches, covered
Paper towel
Decorating bag with tips
2 yards 1-inch-wide pink ribbon

1 Serving (Cake and Frosting): Calories 260 (Calories from Fat 90); Total Fat 10g (Saturated Fat 2.5g; Trans Fat 1.5g); Cholesterol 0mg; Sodium 300mg; Total Carbohydrates 39g (Dietary Fiber 0g; Sugars 24g) • **% Daily Value:** Vitamin A 0%; Vitamin C 0%; Calcium 8%; Iron 6% • **Exchanges:** 1 Starch, 1 1/2 Other Carbohydrates, 2 Fat • **Carbohydrate Choices:** 2 1/2

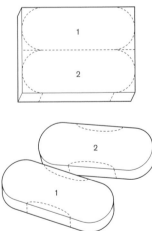

Time-Saver Tip: Substitute 1 box (1 lb 2.25 oz) white cake mix with pudding for the White Cake. Bake as directed for 13 × 9–inch pan. Substitute 2 containers (1 lb each) creamy white frosting for the Creamy White Frosting.

Big Burger Cake

Pound Cake (page 141)

Peanut Butter Frosting (page 146)

2 tablespoons unsweetened baking cocoa

1 to 2 tablespoons strawberry preserves

2 teaspoons toasted sesame seed

1. Bake Pound Cake as directed for 1 1/2-quart round casserole. Cut cake horizontally into 3 equal layers. Freeze pieces uncovered about 1 hour for easier frosting if desired. Make Peanut Butter Frosting. On serving plate, place bottom cake layer. Frost side only.

2. In small bowl, mix 3/4 cup of the remaining frosting and the cocoa; if necessary, stir in 1 to 3 teaspoons milk until spreadable. Frost top of bottom layer with part of the cocoa frosting. Place middle (hamburger) layer on top; frost top and side of middle layer with remaining cocoa frosting.

3. Drizzle preserves over side of middle layer to look like ketchup. Place remaining (rounded) layer on top. Frost with Peanut Butter Frosting. Immediately sprinkle sesame seed over top of cake.

1 Serving (Cake and Frosting): Calories 420 (Calories from Fat 120); Total Fat 13g (Saturated Fat 4g; Trans Fat 1g); Cholesterol 35mg; Sodium 250mg; Total Carbohydrates 70g (Dietary Fiber 1g; Sugars 55g) • **% Daily Value:** Vitamin A 4%; Vitamin C 0%; Calcium 8%; Iron 6% • **Exchanges:** 2 Starch, 2 1/2 Other Carbohydrates, 2 1/2 Fat • **Carbohydrate Choices:** 4 1/2

Personalize It! To really make it look like a burger, sprinkle green-tinted coconut on top of the preserves to look like shredded lettuce before adding the top cake layer.

Time-Saver Tip: Substitute 1 box (1 lb 2.25 oz) cake mix for the Pound Cake. Bake in 1 1/2-quart casserole as directed in recipe. Substitute 2 containers (1 lb each) vanilla creamy frosting, each mixed with 7 drops yellow and 1 drop red food color, for the Peanut Butter Frosting. Substitute 1/2 container (1-lb size) chocolate creamy frosting for the frosting mixed with cocoa.

Kitty Cat Cake

1. Bake White Cake as directed for two 8-inch rounds. Cut cakes as shown in diagram. Freeze pieces uncovered about 1 hour for easier frosting if desired. Make Creamy White Frosting. Put pieces 1 and 2 together with 1/3 cup frosting; on tray, place cut sides down to form body. Attach remaining pieces with about 1 cup frosting to form kitty as shown in diagram, trimming pieces to fit. Frost cake, shaping cheeks and mouth with small spatula.

2. Sprinkle with coconut, pressing gently to adhere. Use shoestring licorice for whiskers. Use jelly beans for nose and eyes. Cut ears and tongue from fruit snack. Use remaining fruit snack to make collar and bow.

White Cake (page 143)

Creamy White Frosting (page 147)

Tray or cardboard, 14 × 11 inches, covered

1 1/2 cups flaked or shredded coconut

Red shoestring licorice

2 blue jelly beans

1 pink jelly bean

1 roll strawberry chewy fruit snack in 3-foot rolls (from 4.5-oz box)

1 Serving (Cake and Frosting): Calories 320 (Calories from Fat 120); Total Fat 13g (Saturated Fat 6g; Trans Fat 1.5g); Cholesterol 0mg; Sodium 330mg; Total Carbohydrates 46g (Dietary Fiber 1g; Sugars 29g) • **% Daily Value:** Vitamin A 0%; Vitamin C 0%; Calcium 10%; Iron 6% • **Exchanges:** 1 Starch, 2 Other Carbohydrates, 2 1/2 Fat • **Carbohydrate Choices:** 3

Time-Saver Tip: Substitute 1 box (1 lb 2.25 oz) white cake mix with pudding for the White Cake. Bake as directed for two 8-inch rounds. Substitute 2 containers (1 lb each) creamy white frosting for the Creamy White Frosting.

Cutting and Assembling Kitty Cat Cake

1. Cut one layer crosswise in half to form body. Frost top of piece 1; top with piece 2.

2. Cut second layer to form legs, head, ears and tail.

3. On tray, place body, cut sides down. Arrange pieces from second layer around body to form kitty.

Snowman Cake

Double-Chocolate Cake (page 140)

Tray or cardboard, 18 × 10 inches, covered

White Mountain Frosting (page 149)

1 cup flaked or shredded coconut

10 small licorice candies

2 blue licorice candies

1 large black gumdrop, cut in half

1 carrot candy or small carrot piece

1 roll chewy fruit snack in 3-foot rolls, any flavor (from 4.5-oz box)

3 chocolate-covered marshmallow cookies

Black shoestring licorice

1 chocolate-covered butter toffee bar

1 pretzel rod

1. Bake Double-Chocolate Cake as directed for one 8-inch round and one 9-inch round. On tray, arrange layers to form snowman. Make White Mountain Frosting. Frost layers, attaching with small amount of frosting.

2. Sprinkle with coconut, pressing gently to adhere. Use small licorice candies for mouth and buttons, blue licorice candies for eyes, black gumdrop for eyebrows, carrot candy for nose and fruit snack for scarf. Cut ends of fruit snack for fringe. Place chocolate-covered cookie on each side of head for earmuffs; attach with shoestring licorice. Cut toffee bar, remaining cookie and pretzel rod in half. Use for legs, shoes and arms.

1 Serving (Cake and Frosting): Calories 450 (Calories from Fat 160); Total Fat 17g (Saturated Fat 8g; Trans Fat 1.5g); Cholesterol 30mg; Sodium 390mg; Total Carbohydrates 69g (Dietary Fiber 2g; Sugars 46g) • **%Daily Value:** Vitamin A 0%; Vitamin C 0%; Calcium 6%; Iron 10% • **Exchanges:** 2 Starch, 2½ Other Carbohydrates, 3 Fat • **Carbohydrate Choices:** 4½

Time-Saver Tip: Substitute 1 box (1 lb 2.25 oz) devil's food cake mix with pudding for the Double-Chocolate Cake. Bake as directed for one 8-inch and one 9-inch round. Substitute 1 box (7.2 oz) fluffy white frosting mix for the White Mountain Frosting.

Dinosaur Cake

1. Bake Yellow Cake as directed for 13 × 9–inch rectangle. Cut cake as shown in diagram. Freeze pieces uncovered about 1 hour for easier frosting if desired. Make Creamy Vanilla Frosting; tint with 6 drops food color. On tray, arrange pieces to form dinosaur as shown in diagram. Frost cake, attaching pieces with small amount of frosting.

2. Let frosting set a few minutes. Carefully cover with a paper towel and gently pat to give frosting a textured appearance; remove towel. Outline scales, legs, mouth, nose and eye with decorating gel. Add jelly bean for eye. Decorate with candy-coated chocolate chips.

Yellow Cake (page 144)

Creamy Vanilla Frosting (page 146)

Green liquid food color

Tray or cardboard, 18 × 12 inches, covered

Paper towel

1 tube (0.68 oz) black or brown decorating gel

Red jelly bean

Green candy-coated chocolate chips

1 Serving (Cake and Frosting): Calories 480 (Calories from Fat 140); Total Fat 16g (Saturated Fat 8g; Trans Fat 1g); Cholesterol 80mg; Sodium 390mg; Total Carbohydrates 80g (Dietary Fiber 0g; Sugars 64g) • **% Daily Value:** Vitamin A 15%; Vitamin C 0%; Calcium 10%; Iron 6% • **Exchanges:** 1 Starch, 4 1/2 Other Carbohydrates, 3 Fat • **Carbohydrate Choices:** 5

Time-Saver Tip: Substitute 1 box (1 lb 2.25 oz) yellow cake mix with pudding for the Yellow Cake. Bake as directed for 13 × 9–inch pan. Substitute 2 containers (1 lb each) creamy vanilla frosting for the Creamy Vanilla Frosting.

Cutting and Assembling Dinosaur Cake

1. Cut cake to form body, feet and tail of dinosaur.

2. Arrange pieces to form dinosaur.

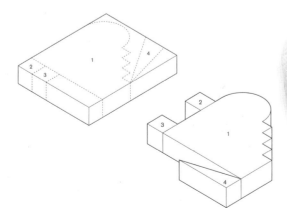

Guitar Cake

1 box (1 lb 2.25 oz) yellow cake mix with pudding

Water, oil and eggs called for on cake mix box

Tray or cardboard, 24 × 16 inches, covered

1 container (1 lb) vanilla creamy frosting

Green and yellow liquid food colors

6 small gumdrops

1 tube (0.68 oz) orange decorating gel

1 thin chocolate wafer cookie

18 tart and tangy small round candies

1 stick gum

Red pull-and-peel licorice

4 multicolored round candies or small gumdrops

1. Heat oven to 350°F. Grease bottom only of 13 × 9–inch pan with shortening or cooking spray. Make cake mix as directed on box, using water, oil and eggs. Pour into pan.

2. Bake 33 to 38 minutes or until toothpick inserted in center comes out clean. Cool 15 minutes. Run knife around sides of pan to loosen cake; remove from pan to wire rack. Cool completely, about 1 hour.

3. Cut 9 × 2–inch strip of cake as shown in diagram for guitar neck. Cut body of guitar from remaining cake. On tray, arrange cake pieces. Freeze pieces uncovered about 1 hour for easier frosting if desired.

4. In small bowl, place ½ cup frosting. Stir in 4 to 6 drops green food color. Stir 6 drops yellow food color into remaining vanilla frosting. Attach guitar neck to body with small amount of frosting; frost top and sides of guitar body with yellow frosting. Frost guitar neck with green frosting. Press 3 gumdrops on each side of neck for tuning pegs. On neck, draw crosswise lines with decorating gel, 1 inch apart, for frets. Place wafer cookie on center of body. Place tart and tangy candies around wafer cookie. Place gum 1 inch under wafer cookie. Place licorice on neck for strings. Press 4 multicolored candies into frosting below gum stick.

1 Serving (Cake and Frosting): Calories 330 (Calories from Fat 140); Total Fat 15g (Saturated Fat 4.5g; Trans Fat 2.5g); Cholesterol 40mg; Sodium 310mg; Total Carbohydrates 45g (Dietary Fiber 0g; Sugars 33g) • **% Daily Value:** Vitamin A 0%; Vitamin C 0%; Calcium 6%; Iron 4% • **Exchanges:** 3 Other Carbohydrates, 3 Fat • **Carbohydrate Choices:** 3

Cutting and Assembling Guitar Cake

1. Cut 9 × 2–inch strip for guitar neck. Cut remaining cake to form guitar body.

2. Arrange guitar and neck pieces.

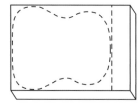
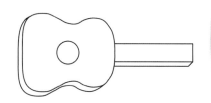

Fish Cake

1. Bake Lemon–Poppy Seed Cake as directed for 13 × 9–inch rectangle. Cut cake as shown in diagram. Freeze pieces uncovered about 1 hour for easier frosting if desired. On tray, arrange pieces to form fish as shown in diagram. Make Creamy Citrus Frosting. Frost cake, attaching pieces with small amount of frosting.

2. To make purple color, in small bowl, mix 5 drops blue food color and 5 drops red food color. Drop purple color along top of fish. Drop 6 drops blue along center and 6 drops yellow along bottom. Starting from top edge of fish, blend colors into frosting with small spatula or spoon, working purple down into blue and blue down into yellow. Use back of spoon to form scales. Define lips with edge of spatula. Mark tail and fins with fork. Use candy for eye.

Lemon–Poppy Seed Cake (page 144)

Tray or cardboard, 18 × 13 inches, covered

Creamy Citrus Frosting (page 146)

Blue, red and yellow liquid food colors

1 round mint candy

1 Serving (Cake and Frosting): Calories 490 (Calories from Fat 150); Total Fat 17g (Saturated Fat 8g; Trans Fat 1g); Cholesterol 80mg; Sodium 390mg; Total Carbohydrates 81g (Dietary Fiber 0g; Sugars 64g) • **% Daily Value:** Vitamin A 15%; Vitamin C 0%; Calcium 10%; Iron 8% • **Exchanges:** 1 Starch, 4¹/₂ Other Carbohydrates, 3 Fat • **Carbohydrate Choices:** 5¹/₂

Personalize It! Get fish lovers hooked on this cake. Create a big pond by covering the board with blue plastic wrap and decorating with green decorating gel or frosting for seaweed. Add sea creatures and shells to complete the look.

Cutting and Assembling Fish Cake

1. Cut cake to form body, fins and mouth of fish.

2. Arrange pieces to form fish.

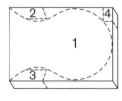

Time-Saver Tip: Substitute 1 box (1 lb 2.25 oz) yellow cake mix with pudding for the Lemon–Poppy Seed Cake. Bake as directed for 13 × 9–inch pan. Substitute 2 containers (1 lb each) vanilla creamy frosting for the Creamy Citrus Frosting.

Gum Ball Machine Cake

1 box (1 lb 2.25 oz) white cake mix
  with pudding

1¼ cups bubble gum–flavored
  soda pop or water

⅓ cup vegetable oil

3 egg whites

Red or blue food color (to match color
  of soda pop), if desired

Tray or cardboard, 24 × 16 inches,
  covered

1 container (12 oz) vanilla whipped
  frosting

1 teaspoon red or blue liquid or paste
  food color

1 bar (1.5 oz) chocolate-covered
  crispy candy

1 tube (0.68 oz) blue decorating gel

1 foil-covered chocolate coin

1 peanut-shaped candy

Gum balls

1. Heat oven to 350°F. Grease bottoms only of one 8-inch or 9-inch round pan and one 8-inch square pan with shortening or with cooking spray. In large bowl, beat cake mix, soda pop, oil, egg whites and a few drops food color with electric mixer on low speed 30 seconds. Beat on medium speed 2 minutes, scraping bowl occasionally. Divide batter evenly between pans.

2. Bake 23 to 33 minutes or until toothpick inserted in center comes out clean (times may vary between the two pans). Cool 10 minutes. Run knife around sides of pans to loosen cakes; remove from pans to wire rack. Cool completely, about 1 hour. Freeze cakes uncovered about 1 hour for easier frosting if desired.

3. On tray, place round cake near one end for globe of gum ball machine; frost top and sides with half of the frosting. Place cake square next to globe for machine base. Stir 1 teaspoon food color into remaining frosting; frost sides and top of base with frosting. Wrap candy bar with foil. Place foil-wrapped candy bar near bottom of base. Use decorating gel to draw trap door on candy bar. Arrange chocolate coin and peanut candy above candy bar. Arrange gum balls on globe.

1 Serving (Cake and Frosting): Calories 280 (Calories from Fat 110); Total Fat 12g (Saturated Fat 3g; Trans Fat 0.5g); Cholesterol 0mg; Sodium 250mg; Total Carbohydrates 40g (Dietary Fiber 0g; Sugars 28g) • **% Daily Value:** Vitamin A 0%; Vitamin C 0%; Calcium 4%; Iron 4% • **Exchanges:** 2½ Other Carbohydrates, 2½ Fat • **Carbohydrate Choices:** 2½

Personalize It! Instead of using the candy bar, you can "draw" the trapdoor on the cake with decorating icing or gel.

Monkey Cake

Dark Cocoa Cake (page 139)

Creamy Cocoa Frosting (page 146)

1 tablespoon powdered sugar

Tray or cardboard, 16 × 14 inches, covered

Decorating bag with tips

2 banana chips

2 semisweet chocolate chips

1 pecan half

1 dwarf banana

1. Bake Dark Cocoa Cake as directed for 13 × 9–inch rectangle. Cut cake as shown in diagram. Freeze pieces uncovered about 1 hour for easier frosting if desired. Make Creamy Cocoa Frosting. In small bowl, reserve 2 tablespoons frosting; stir in powdered sugar and reserve.

2. On tray, arrange pieces to form monkey as shown in diagram; trim pieces 2 and 3 to fit for arms. Frost sides and top of cake with cocoa frosting, attaching pieces with small amount of frosting. Make lines in frosting with tines of fork to look like fur, leaving face area smooth.

3. Place reserved frosting in decorating bag fitted with writing tip #4. Pipe outlines of face and hands. Add banana chips for eyes, attaching chocolate chips in center with small amount of frosting. Add pecan half for nose. Place banana in monkey's hand.

1 Serving (Cake and Frosting): Calories 460 (Calories from Fat 160); Total Fat 18g (Saturated Fat 6g; Trans Fat 2g); Cholesterol 45mg; Sodium 320mg; Total Carbohydrates 68g (Dietary Fiber 3g; Sugars 50g) • **% Daily Value:** Vitamin A 6%; Vitamin C 0%; Calcium 2%; Iron 10% • **Exchanges:** 1 Starch, 3 1/2 Other Carbohydrates, 3 1/2 Fat • **Carbohydrate Choices:** 4 1/2

Time-Saver Tip: Substitute 1 box (1 lb 2.25 oz) devil's food cake mix with pudding for the Dark Cocoa Cake. Bake as directed for 13 × 9–inch pan. Substitute 1 1/2 containers (1 lb each) chocolate creamy frosting for the Creamy Cocoa Frosting.

Cutting and Assembling Monkey Cake

1. Cut cake to form body and arms.

2. Arrange pieces to form monkey.

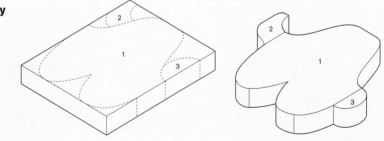

Panda Cake

Marble Cake (page 143)

Tray or cardboard, 16 × 10 inches, covered

White Mountain Frosting (page 149)

½ cup flaked coconut

8 thin chocolate wafer cookies, about 2 inches in diameter

1 large marshmallow

2 chocolate-covered candies

1 small black or red gumdrop

Black shoestring licorice

⅓ cup flaked coconut

1 teaspoon unsweetened baking cocoa

1. Bake Marble Cake as directed for one 8-inch round and one 9-inch round. Cut 9-inch round as shown in diagram. Freeze pieces uncovered about 1 hour for easier frosting if desired. On tray, arrange pieces to form panda as shown in diagram.

2. Make White Mountain Frosting. Frost cake, attaching pieces with small amount of frosting. Sprinkle body with ½ cup flaked coconut, pressing gently to adhere. Press 2 wafers into top of head at 45° angle for ears. Place 2 wafers for background of eyes and 4 on body for paws, placing bottom 2 wafers at 45° angle on bottom edge of cake.

3. Cut marshmallow crosswise in half; place each half on a chocolate wafer for eyes. Place chocolate candies on marshmallow halves for pupils; fasten with small dab of frosting if necessary. Use small gumdrop for nose and shoestring licorice for mouth and outline of legs. In small bowl, toss ⅓ cup coconut and the cocoa; carefully sprinkle within outlines of legs and on bottom portion of body.

1 Serving (Cake and Frosting): Calories 330 (Calories from Fat 110); Total Fat 12g (Saturated Fat 3.5g; Trans Fat 1.5g); Cholesterol 0mg; Sodium 330mg; Total Carbohydrates 51g (Dietary Fiber 1g; Sugars 33g) • **% Daily Value:** Vitamin A 0%; Vitamin C 0%; Calcium 10%; Iron 8% • **Exchanges:** 1 Starch, 2½ Other Carbohydrates, 2½ Fat • **Carbohydrate Choices:** 3½

Time-Saver Tip: Substitute 1 box (1 lb 2.25 oz) fudge marble or devil's food cake mix with pudding for the Marble Cake. Bake as directed for one 8-inch round and one 9-inch round. Substitute 1 box (7.2 oz) fluffy white frosting mix for the White Mountain Frosting. Prepare as directed on box.

Cutting and Assembling Panda Cake

1. Cut small curved piece from one side of 9-inch layer.

2. Join 8-inch layer to cut section of cake 1.

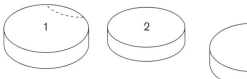

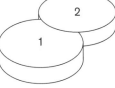

Teddy Bear Cake

1. Bake Double-Chocolate Cake as directed for one 8-inch round and one 9-inch square. Cut cake as shown in diagram. Freeze pieces uncovered about 1 hour for easier frosting if desired. Make Creamy Chocolate Frosting; reserve 2 tablespoons. On tray, arrange cake pieces to form a teddy bear as shown in diagram. Frost cake, attaching pieces with small amount of frosting.

2. Make fur marks in frosting with fork, leaving face smooth. Cut tongue, ears and bow from fruit snack. Use black gumdrops for eyes, one large red gumdrop for nose and licorice for mouth. Accent bow with other large red gumdrop. Sprinkle nonpareils on cheeks and paws. Use 3 small gumdrop halves for pads on each paw. Position ice-cream cone, cut side down, between top paws for honey pot. Place reserved frosting in decorating bag fitted with writing tip #3. Pipe "Honey" on cone.

Double-Chocolate Cake (page 140)

Creamy Chocolate Frosting (page 146)

Tray or cardboard, 17 × 12 inches, covered

1 roll strawberry chewy fruit snack in 3-foot rolls (from 4.5-oz box)

2 large black gumdrops

2 large red gumdrops

Red shoestring licorice

Pink nonpareil candies

6 small red gumdrops, cut in half

Decorating bag with tips

1/2 ice-cream cone

1 Serving (Cake and Frosting): Calories 520 (Calories from Fat 210); Total Fat 23g (Saturated Fat 10g; Trans Fat 1.5g); Cholesterol 45mg; Sodium 360mg; Total Carbohydrates 73g (Dietary Fiber 3g; Sugars 54g) • % Daily Value: Vitamin A 6%; Vitamin C 0%; Calcium 6%; Iron 10% • Exchanges: 1 Starch, 4 Other Carbohydrates, 4 1/2 Fat • Carbohydrate Choices: 5

Personalize It! You can use a lollipop, candy cane or other candy instead of the ice-cream cone, or you can eliminate it altogether.

Cutting and Assembling Teddy Bear Cake

1. Cut small piece from side of round cake.

2. Cut square cake to form body and ears.

3. Arrange pieces to form teddy bear.

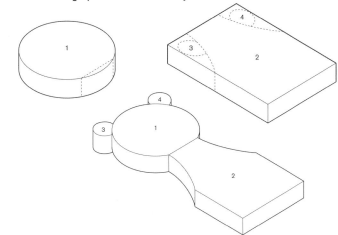

Play Ball Cake

2 recipes Yellow Cake (page 144)

Creamy White Frosting (page 147)

Tray or cardboard, 15 inches round, covered

Red shoestring licorice

Decorating gel (from 0.68-oz tube)

Baseball Caps (page 35)

Bake 1 recipe Yellow Cake as directed for 2-quart round casserole. Repeat with second recipe. Make Creamy White Frosting. On tray, place 1 cake, rounded side down. Trim top to make a flat surface. Spread with ⅓ cup frosting. Trim top of second layer flat. Place upside down on top of first layer to make a ball. Frost entire cake. Use red licorice for seams on baseball. Pipe desired message with decorating gel. Arrange Baseball Caps around baseball.

1 Serving (Cake and Frosting): Calories 230 (Calories from Fat 70); Total Fat 8g (Saturated Fat 3.5g; Trans Fat 0g); Cholesterol 60mg; Sodium 330mg; Total Carbohydrates 36g (Dietary Fiber 0g; Sugars 22g) • **% Daily Value:** Vitamin A 6%; Vitamin C 0%; Calcium 10%; Iron 6% • **Exchanges:** 1 Starch, 1½ Other Carbohydrates, 1½ Fat • **Carbohydrate Choices:** 2½

Personalize It! Feed the whole team with this cake! Or omit the Baseball Caps if you want just the ball. To make a basketball, tint the frosting orange and use string licorice for a basketball design. For a soccer ball, outline the design with a toothpick and fill in every other section with desired colored frostings.

Time-Saver Tip: Substitute 2 boxes (1 lb 2.25 oz each) yellow cake mix with pudding for the Yellow Cake. Bake as directed in Yellow Cake recipe for 2-quart round casserole. Substitute 1 box (1 lb 2.25 oz) devil's food cake mix with pudding for the Double-Chocolate Cake in the Baseball Caps recipe. Bake as directed on box for cupcakes. Substitute 4 containers (1 oz each) creamy white frosting for the Creamy White Frosting.

Baseball Caps

Bake Double-Chocolate Cake as directed for muffin cups to make cupcakes. Make Creamy White Frosting. Divide frosting among small bowls for as many colors as desired. Stir 2 drops desired food color into frosting in each bowl. Trim top of each cupcake to make a flat surface. Frost bottoms and sides of cupcakes with assorted colored frostings. Place as many cupcakes around baseball as will fit. Place remaining cupcakes on separate tray. Starting at center top of each cap, place pieces of licorice down sides for seams. Place 1 candy-coated fruit piece at center top. Use fruit slices for brims (trim fruit slices if necessary). Pipe child's name or team initial on caps with decorating gel.

Double-Chocolate Cake (page 140)

Creamy White Frosting (page 147)

Assorted liquid food colors

Black shoestring licorice

Candy-coated fruit pieces

Assorted candied fruit slices

Decorating gel (from 0.68-oz tube)

1 Cupcake (Cake and Frosting): Calories 210 (Calories from Fat 80); Total Fat 9g (Saturated Fat 3.5g; Trans Fat 1g); Cholesterol 20mg; Sodium 200mg; Total Carbohydrates 30g (Dietary Fiber 1g; Sugars 20g) • **% Daily Value:** Vitamin A 0%; Vitamin C 0%; Calcium 4%; Iron 6% • **Exchanges:** 1 Starch, 1 Other Carbohydrates, 1½ Fat • **Carbohydrate Choices:** 2

Sailboat Cake

1 box (1 lb 2.25 oz) cake mix
   with pudding

Water, oil and eggs called for
   on cake mix box

Tray or cardboard, 24 × 24 inches,
   covered

1 container (12 oz) fluffy white
   whipped frosting

1 tablespoon unsweetened baking
   cocoa

1 red licorice twist

1 roll chewy fruit snack in 3-foot rolls,
   any flavor (from 4.5-oz box)

Ring-shaped hard candies

Tiny star candies

Miniature candy-coated chocolate
   baking bits

1. Heat oven to 350°F. Grease bottom only of 13 × 9–inch pan with shortening or cooking spray. Make cake mix as directed on box, using water, oil and eggs. Pour into pan.

2. Bake cake as directed on box for 13 × 9–inch pan. Cool 15 minutes. Run knife around side of pan to loosen cake; remove from pan to wire rack. Cool completely, about 1 hour.

3. Cut cake as shown in diagram. Freeze pieces uncovered about 1 hour for easier frosting if desired. On tray, arrange cake pieces to form sailboat as shown in diagram, leaving space between sails for mast. Frost sails with 1 cup frosting.

4. Gently fold cocoa into remaining frosting until blended. Frost hull of sailboat with cocoa frosting. Place piece of licorice on cake for mast between sails. Cut flags from fruit snack and press on mast. Decorate cake with candies.

1 Serving (Cake and Frosting): Calories 300 (Calories from Fat 120); Total Fat 14g (Saturated Fat 3g; Trans Fat 0.5g); Cholesterol 40mg; Sodium 260mg; Total Carbohydrates 42g (Dietary Fiber 0g; Sugars 29g) • % Daily Value: Vitamin A 0%; Vitamin C 0%; Calcium 6%; Iron 4% • Exchanges: 1 Starch, 2 Other Carbohydrates, 2½ Fat • Carbohydrate Choices: 3

Personalize It! Check your pantry for candies you may have on hand to create a sailing scene. Decorate the tray with sun and bird shapes, using frosting to keep them in place, or create the shapes with frosting.

Cutting and Assembling Sailboat Cake

1. Cut cake diagonally into 3 pieces.

2. Arrange pieces to form sailboat, leaving space between sails for mast.

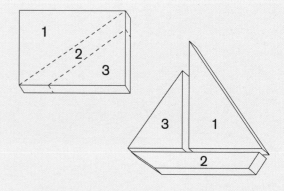

Space Shuttle Cake

Yellow Cake (page 144)

Creamy Vanilla Frosting (page 146)

Tray or cardboard, 17 × 12 inches, covered

Red string licorice

Red and blue miniature candy-coated chocolate baking bits

2 red gumdrop stars

3 small candy stars

6 soft red round candies

1 tube (0.68 oz) blue decorating gel

3 candles

1. Bake Yellow Cake as directed for 13 × 9–inch rectangle. Cut cake as shown in diagram. Freeze pieces uncovered about 1 hour for easier frosting if desired. Make Creamy Vanilla Frosting.

2. On tray, place cake piece 1. Frost with about 1¼ cups frosting. Arrange pieces 2, 3 and 4 as shown in diagram, trimming to fit, standing up piece 3 for top fin. Trim point of piece 2 for nose of shuttle. Frost cake with remaining frosting.

3. Use licorice to make diagonal lines across nose of shuttle and to outline top fin. Use baking bits to outline tip, wings and back of shuttle. Add large and small stars to wings and back; add round candies to both sides of fin. Write "USA" or another message on top of fin with gel. Insert candles at end of shuttle. Just before serving, light candles for "liftoff" if desired.

1 Serving (Cake and Frosting): Calories 480 (Calories from Fat 140); Total Fat 16g (Saturated Fat 8g; Trans Fat 1g); Cholesterol 80mg; Sodium 390mg; Total Carbohydrates 80g (Dietary Fiber 0g; Sugars 64g) • **% Daily Value:** Vitamin A 15%; Vitamin C 0%; Calcium 10%; Iron 6% • **Exchanges:** 1 Starch, 4½ Other Carbohydrates, 3 Fat • **Carbohydrate Choices:** 5

Cutting and Assembling Space Shuttle Cake

1. Cut cake to form body pieces of shuttle.

2. Place piece 1 on tray; frost. Arrange remaining pieces to form shuttle, standing up piece 3 for top fin.

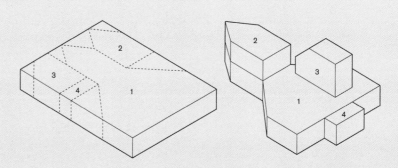

Time-Saver Tip: Substitute 1 box (1 lb 2.25 oz) yellow cake mix with pudding for the Yellow Cake. Bake as directed for 13 × 9–inch pan. Substitute 2 containers (1 lb each) vanilla creamy frosting for the Creamy Vanilla Frosting.

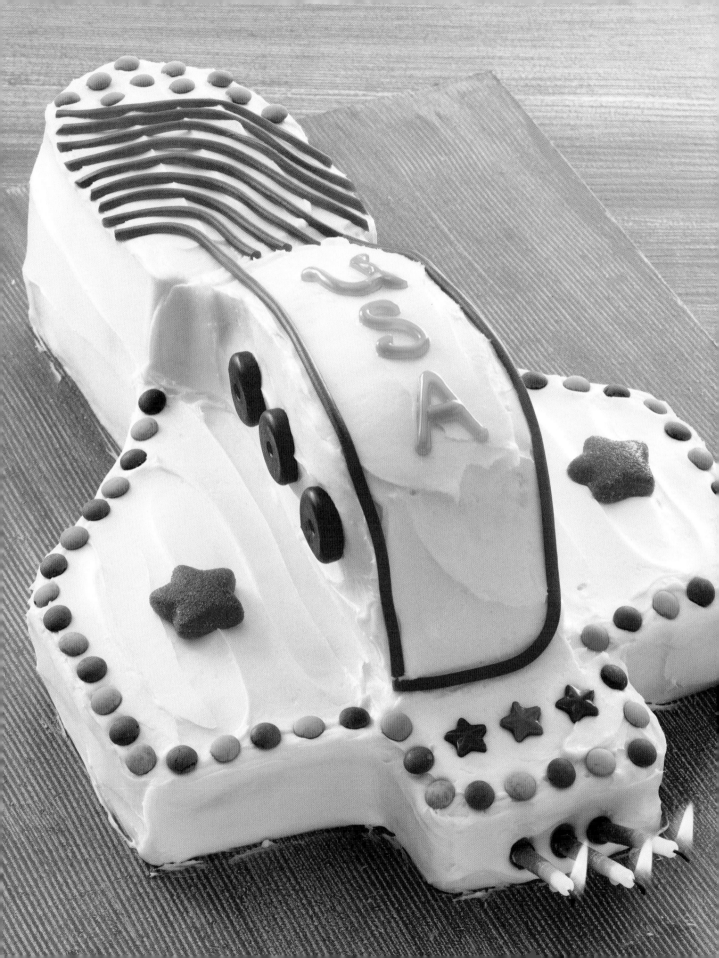

Train Cake

Double-Chocolate Cake (page 140)

Creamy Chocolate Frosting (page 146)

Tray or cardboard, 25 × 13 inches, covered

String licorice

Gumdrops

2 creme-filled chocolate sandwich cookies

Jelly beans

Creamy Vanilla Frosting (page 146)

Paste or gel food colors in desired colors

Peach gummy candy rings

1. Bake Double-Chocolate Cake as directed for two 9 × 5–inch loaves. Cut cake as shown in diagram, being careful not to cut all the way through piece 1 when removing piece 2. Trim pieces 3, 4, 5 and 6 to be flat on top. Freeze pieces uncovered about 1 hour for easier frosting. Make Creamy Chocolate Frosting.

2. On tray, place piece 1 for engine, stacking piece 2 on top for engine house, as shown in diagram. Frost with chocolate frosting. Cut strips of licorice; place on front of engine, slanting outward, for the cowcatcher. Add gumdrops for engine "face." Attach cookies at back of engine with small amount of frosting. Top the engine with jelly beans; add strips of licorice to sides of engine.

3. Make Creamy Vanilla Frosting. Divide frosting into fourths. Tint each fourth with different color of food color. Place remaining cake pieces on tray for boxcars. Frost each with a different color of frosting. Top cars with jelly beans; add strips of licorice to sides of cars. Add gummy candy rings for wheels.

1 Serving (Cake and Frosting): Calories 770 (Calories from Fat 280); Total Fat 31g (Saturated Fat 15g; Trans Fat 2g); Cholesterol 70mg; Sodium 410mg; Total Carbohydrates 117g (Dietary Fiber 3g; Sugars 97g) • **% Daily Value:** Vitamin A 10%; Vitamin C 0%; Calcium 6%; Iron 10% • **Exchanges:** 2 Starch, 5½ Other Carbohydrates, 6 Fat • **Carbohydrate Choices:** 8

Cutting and Assembling Train Cake

1. Cut narrow strip lengthwise from each side of one loaf. Remove a 1½-inch-wide, 1½-inch-thick section from piece 1, being careful not to cut all the way through.

2. Place piece 2 on top of piece 1 for engine house.

3. Cut second loaf crosswise into fourths; place each piece behind engine for boxcars.

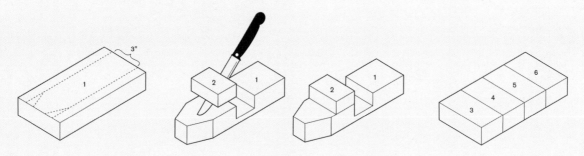

Time-Saver Tip: Substitute 1 box (1 lb 2.25 oz) chocolate fudge cake mix with pudding for the Double-Chocolate Cake. Prepare as directed on box—except bake as directed in Double-Chocolate Cake recipe for 9 × 5–inch loaf pans. Substitute 1 container (1 lb) chocolate creamy frosting for the Creamy Chocolate Frosting and 2 containers (1 lb each) vanilla creamy frosting for the Creamy Vanilla Frosting.

Little Red Barn Cake

1 box (1 lb 2.25 oz) white cake mix
    with pudding

1¼ cups water

⅓ cup vegetable oil

2 large eggs

Tray or cardboard, 17 × 12 inches,
    covered

1 to 2 teaspoons red paste food color

1 container (1 lb) vanilla creamy frosting

3 rectangular buttery crackers

8 pretzel sticks (3 inches long)

½ cup vanilla creamy frosting
    (from 1-lb container)

Decorating bag with tips

2 tablespoons coconut

Green liquid food color

2 tablespoons shoestring potatoes
    (from 1.75-oz can)

3 or 4 animal crackers

1. Heat oven to 350°F. Grease bottom and sides of 15 × 10 × 1-inch pan with shortening. Line bottom of pan with waxed paper. Lightly grease waxed paper; lightly flour. In large bowl, beat cake mix, water, oil and eggs with electric mixer on low speed until moistened. Beat on medium speed 2 minutes. Pour into pan.

2. Bake 20 to 30 minutes or until toothpick inserted in center comes out clean. Cool cake 5 minutes; remove from pan to wire rack. Peel off waxed paper. Cool completely, about 45 minutes. Freeze cake 30 minutes or until very firm.

3. Place cake on cutting board. Cut cake as shown in diagram to make roof line and silo. Carefully transfer cake to tray. Stir red paste food color into 1 container of frosting to make desired red color. Frost barn and silo—except for upper rounded section—with red frosting. Make vertical lines over cake with rubber spatula to look like boards.

4. Place 2 crackers side by side on barn for doors. Place 1 cracker at an angle under peak of barn for window; press into frosting. Arrange pretzel sticks around window and door; make an X shape on each door with remaining pretzel sticks. Spoon ½ cup vanilla frosting into decorating bag fitted with small star tip. Pipe vanilla frosting along edge of roof and fill in top rounded section of silo.

5. In resealable food-storage plastic bag, shake coconut and 2 drops green food color until coconut is evenly tinted. Arrange coconut along bottom edge of cake for grass. Arrange shoestring potatoes in window and at bottom of cake for hay. Place animal crackers on cake above grass.

1 Serving (Cake and Frosting): Calories 370 (Calories from Fat 160); Total Fat 18g (Saturated Fat 5g; Trans Fat 3.5g); Cholesterol 30mg; Sodium 330mg; Total Carbohydrates 50g (Dietary Fiber 0g; Sugars 37g) • **% Daily Value:** Vitamin A 0%; Vitamin C 0%; Calcium 4%; Iron 4% • **Exchanges:** 1 Starch, 2½ Other Carbohydrates, 3½ Fat • **Carbohydrate Choices:** 3

Cut cake to form barn and silo.

Design It! STENCILS

- Cut stencils from lightweight cardboard, waxed paper or sheets of plastic cut to the size of the cake. Or use doilies or purchased stencils.

- Place stencil on unfrosted, frosted or glazed cake. (Allow frostings and glazes to set before stenciling.) Sift cocoa, powdered sugar, ground cinnamon or nutmeg, colored sugars or gelatin over stencil.

- Carefully remove stencil to show design. For more intricate designs, use two or three colors of sifted ingredients.

Butterfly Cake

1 box (1 lb 2.25 oz) yellow cake mix with pudding

Water, oil and eggs called for on cake mix box

Tray or cardboard, 16 × 16 inches, covered

1 container (1 lb) vanilla creamy frosting

1 striped candy stick (8 to 10 inches long)

Food colors (in desired colors)

Decorating gel (from 0.68-oz tube) in any color

Decorator sugar crystals (any color)

8 jelly beans

Small round candy decorations

1. Heat oven to 350°F. Grease bottom and side of one 8- or 9-inch round pan with shortening; lightly flour. Make cake mix as directed on box, using water, oil and eggs. Pour half of the batter into pan.*

2. Bake 35 to 40 minutes or until toothpick inserted in center comes out clean. Cool cake 15 minutes; remove from pan to wire rack. Cool completely, about 30 minutes. Freeze cake 1 hour or until firm.

3. Cut cake crosswise in half; cut each half into ⅓ and ⅔ pieces as shown in diagram. On tray, arrange cake pieces to form butterfly as shown in diagram. Gently separate cake pieces to form wings.

4. Reserve ½ cup frosting. Frost cake pieces with remaining frosting. Place candy stick between cake pieces for butterfly body. Stir food color into reserved frosting until well blended; spread over cake in desired pattern on wings. Outline wing patterns with gel. Sprinkle with sugar crystals. Place jelly beans on corners of wings. Decorate butterfly with candy decorations.

Use remaining batter for cupcakes. Place paper baking cup in each of 12 regular-size muffin cups. Divide batter evenly among cups. Bake at 350°F for 20 to 30 minutes or until toothpick inserted in center comes out clean. Remove from pan to wire rack; cool completely. Frost and decorate as desired.

1 Serving (Cake and Frosting): Calories 290 (Calories from Fat 130); Total Fat 14g (Saturated Fat 4.5g; Trans Fat 3g); Cholesterol 25mg; Sodium 240mg; Total Carbohydrates 39g (Dietary Fiber 0g; Sugars 31g) • **% Daily Value:** Vitamin A 0%; Vitamin C 0%; Calcium 4%; Iron 2% • **Exchanges:** ½ Starch, 2 Other Carbohydrates, 3 Fat • **Carbohydrate Choices:** 2½

Cutting and Assembling Butterfly Cake

1. Cut cake crosswise in half; cut each half into ⅓ and ⅔ pieces.

2. On tray, arrange cake pieces to form butterfly.

3. Separate cake pieces to form wings.

Inchworm Cake

1. Heat oven to 350°F. Grease 12-cup fluted tube cake pan with shortening. Make cake mix as directed on box, using water, oil and eggs. Pour into pan.

2. Bake as directed on box or until toothpick inserted in center comes out clean. Cool 15 minutes; remove from pan to wire rack. Cool completely, about 1 hour.

3. Cut cake as shown in diagram. Freeze pieces uncovered about 1 hour for easier frosting. Stir food color into frosting. On tray, arrange cake pieces to form inchworm as shown in diagram. Frost cake, attaching pieces with frosting.

4. Attach 1 chocolate candy to each vanilla wafer with frosting; attach to end of cake for eyes. Press 3 candies into frosting for mouth. Gently push 1 pretzel stick into flat end of gumdrop; repeat with second pretzel stick. Insert pretzel sticks into cake for antennae. Arrange remaining gumdrops along edge for feet.

1 box (1 lb 2.25 oz) cake mix with pudding

Water, oil and eggs called for on cake mix box

8 drops green liquid food color

1½ containers (1 lb each) vanilla creamy frosting

Tray or cardboard, 19 × 14 inches, covered

5 candy-coated chocolate candies

2 vanilla wafer cookies

2 small pretzel sticks

24 small gumdrops

1 Serving (Cake and Frosting): Calories 400 (Calories from Fat 170); Total Fat 19g (Saturated Fat 6g; Trans Fat 4g); Cholesterol 40mg; Sodium 350mg; Total Carbohydrates 53g (Dietary Fiber 0g; Sugars 40g) • **% Daily Value:** Vitamin A 0%; Vitamin C 0%; Calcium 4%; Iron 4% • **Exchanges:** 1 Starch, 2½ Other Carbohydrates, 3½ Fat • **Carbohydrate Choices:** 3½

Cutting and Assembling Inchworm Cake

1. Cut cake as shown by dotted lines.

2. Stand large cake piece on cut end. Arrange pieces 1 and 2 on ends of large cake piece.

Ladybug Cake

1 box (1 lb 2.25 oz) yellow or white cake mix with pudding

1¼ cups water

⅓ cup vegetable oil

3 large eggs

1 container (12 oz) fluffy white whipped frosting

Red paste food color

½ container (1-lb size) milk chocolate creamy frosting

Black licorice wheels

2 red cinnamon candies

1 raspberry nonpareil-covered chewy candy

Chocolate sprinkles

1. Heat oven to 350°F. Generously grease bottom only of 1½-quart round casserole or heatproof bowl with shortening. Grease bottom only of four 6-ounce custard cups with shortening.

2. In large bowl, beat cake mix, water, oil and eggs with electric mixer on low speed 30 seconds. Beat on medium speed 2 minutes, scraping bowl constantly. Pour two-thirds of the batter into casserole; pour remaining batter into custard cups.

3. Bake about 40 minutes or until toothpick inserted in center comes out clean. Cool 10 minutes. Run knife around sides of casserole and custard cups to loosen cakes; remove from casserole and cups to wire rack. Cool completely, about 1 hour. Wrap and freeze 3 small rounds for another use.

4. On serving plate, place large cake with rounded side up. Tint white frosting with food color. Frost body of ladybug with red frosting. Add small cake for head; frost with chocolate frosting. Uncoil a licorice wheel; place down center of ladybug body. Add licorice wheels for spots.

5. Add cinnamon candies to head for eyes. Add raspberry candy for nose. Sprinkle chocolate sprinkles over head. Add pieces of licorice for legs and antennae.

1 Serving (Cake and Frosting): Calories 300 (Calories from Fat 120); Total Fat 14g (Saturated Fat 3g; Trans Fat 0.5g); Cholesterol 40mg; Sodium 260mg; Total Carbohydrates 41g (Dietary Fiber 0g; Sugars 29g) • **% Daily Value:** Vitamin A 0%; Vitamin C 0%; Calcium 6%; Iron 4% • **Exchanges:** 1 Starch, 2 Other Carbohydrates, 2½ Fat • **Carbohydrate Choices:** 3

Purse Cake

1. Heat oven to 350°F. Grease bottom only of 13 × 9–inch pan with shortening or cooking spray. In large bowl, mix cake mix, water, oil and egg whites as directed on box. Pour batter into pan.

2. Bake as directed on box for 13 × 9–inch pan. Cool 10 minutes; remove from pan to wire rack. Cool completely, about 30 minutes.

3. Cut cake crosswise in half. On serving plate, place 1 cake piece; spread with 2 tablespoons white frosting. Top with second cake piece. Stand cake pieces on end with cut side down. Freeze 1 hour.

4. Stir food color into 1 container of frosting to tint light blue. Spread entire cake with light blue frosting. Along front and top of cake, mark outline of an elongated V-shape with toothpick for purse flap. Stir food color into remaining ½ container of frosting to tint dark blue; frost purse flap with dark blue frosting. Place remaining dark blue frosting in decorating bag fitted with writing tips #7 or #8; pipe shell border along purse flap and edges of purse.

5. Cut rim from plastic plate; cut rim in half. Insert into top of cake for handle. Decorate purse with candies. Cut marshmallow with dampened kitchen scissors into slices; sprinkle with colored sugar. Arrange on purse for clasp. Press candy onto center of clasp.

1 box (1 lb 2.25 oz) white cake mix with pudding

Water, oil and egg whites called for on cake mix box

1½ containers (1 lb each) creamy white frosting

Blue paste food color

Decorating bag with tips

1 plastic plate

Candy-coated chocolate candies

1 or 2 large marshmallows

Colored sugar

1 Serving (Cake and Frosting): Calories 390 (Calories from Fat 160); Total Fat 18g (Saturated Fat 6g; Trans Fat 4g); Cholesterol 0mg; Sodium 350mg; Total Carbohydrates 53g (Dietary Fiber 0g; Sugars 40g) • **% Daily Value:** Vitamin A 0%; Vitamin C 0%; Calcium 4%; Iron 4% • **Exchanges:** 1 Starch, 2½ Other Carbohydrates, 3½ Fat • **Carbohydrate Choices:** 3½

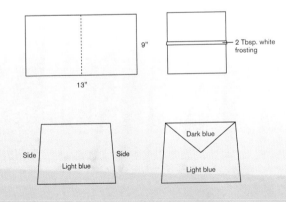

Personalize It! Choose from the many colorful candies available to decorate this adorable cake.

Castle Cake

2 boxes (1 lb 2.25 oz each) chocolate fudge cake mix with pudding

Water, oil and eggs called for on cake mix boxes

Tray or cardboard, 18 × 18 inches, covered

2 containers (1 lb each) milk chocolate creamy frosting

1 fudge-dipped ice-cream cone

4 regular-size ice-cream cones with pointed ends

5 miniature ice-cream cones with pointed ends

1 tube (4.25 oz) white decorating icing

Blue colored sugar

Candy stars

5 rectangular vanilla sugar wafer cookies

Pretzel sticks

4 red cinnamon candies

Red string licorice

4 miniature peanut butter cup candies

4 red juju cocktail candies

4 white gum balls

12 miniature chocolate-covered caramels

1. Heat oven to 350°F. Grease bottoms and sides of four 8-inch square pans with shortening or cooking spray. In large bowl, mix both cake mixes with water, oil and eggs for both mixes as directed on box. Divide batter among pans (about 2⅓ cups for each pan). Refrigerate 2 pans of batter while 2 pans bake.

2. Bake 2 pans at a time, following times on cake mix box for 8-inch round pans. Cool 10 minutes; remove from pans to wire racks. Cool completely, about 30 minutes.

3. Cut off domed top from each cake so they will be flat when stacked. On tray, place cake A; spread with ⅓ cup chocolate frosting. Top with cake B; spread with ⅓ cup chocolate frosting. Top with cake C; spread with ⅓ cup chocolate frosting.

4. Cut fourth cake into quarters. Place one quarter on top of stacked cakes (piece 1); spread top with 1 tablespoon chocolate frosting. Cut second quarter horizontally in half; place half of second quarter on top of first quarter (piece 2) and spread top with 1 tablespoon chocolate frosting. Cut third quarter into 2-inch square (piece 3); place on center of cake stack. Freeze 1 hour. (Discard remaining cake or reserve for another use.)

5. Reserve 2 tablespoons frosting in resealable food-storage plastic bag. Spread remaining chocolate frosting over entire stacked cake. Place fudge-dipped cone upside down on center of castle. Place 4 regular ice-cream cones upside down on corners of cake.

6. Dip edges of miniature cones in white decorating icing; sprinkle with colored sugar. Place upside down on top of larger cones. Top each cone with candy star, attaching with small amount of white icing.

7. Cut 1 wafer cookie in half. Snip tiny corner from bag of frosting; pipe frosting on 2 whole and 1 half cookies for window panes. Place windows on castle. Insert ends of pretzels slightly into cake for drawbridge. Place 2 cookies on drawbridge for door; press tops slightly against cake. Add cinnamon candies to doors and front of cake. Add licorice for bridge wire.

8. Place peanut butter cup candies upside down on 4 corners near top of castle. Add red juju candies and gum balls to peanut butter candies with small amount of white icing to make turrets. Add caramels to front of cake for parapets.

1 Serving (Cake and Frosting): Calories 300 (Calories from Fat 100); Total Fat 11g (Saturated Fat 3g; Trans Fat 2.5g); Cholesterol 20mg; Sodium 360mg; Total Carbohydrates 47g (Dietary Fiber 0g; Sugars 33g) • **% Daily Value:** Vitamin A 0%; Vitamin C 0%; Calcium 4%; Iron 10% • **Exchanges:** 1 Starch, 2 Other Carbohydrates, 2 Fat • **Carbohydrate Choices:** 3

Flip-Flops Cake

1 box (1 lb 2.25 oz) yellow cake mix with pudding

Water, oil and eggs called for on cake mix box

Tray or cardboard, 20 × 18 inches, covered

2 cups vanilla whipped frosting (from two 12-oz containers)

Paste or gel food colors

About 40 small round candy-coated fruit-flavored chewy candies

Assorted colors of decorating icing (in 4.25-oz tubes)

1 roll chewy fruit snack in 3-foot rolls, any flavor (from 4.5-oz box)

2 silk daisy flowers

1. Heat oven to 350°F. Grease bottom only of 13 × 9–inch pan with shortening or cooking spray. Make cake mix as directed on box, using water, oil and eggs. Pour into pan.

2. Bake 33 to 38 minutes or until toothpick inserted in center comes out clean. Cool 15 minutes. Run knife around sides of pan to loosen cake; remove from pan to wire rack. Cool completely, about 1 hour.

3. Cut cake lengthwise in half. Continue cutting each piece to form flip-flop shape as shown in diagram. Freeze pieces uncovered about 1 hour for easier frosting if desired.

4. On tray, arrange cake pieces. For one color of flip-flops, tint frosting with one food color. For two-tone flip-flops, in small bowl, mix 1 cup of the frosting with food color to make desired color; frost sides of each flip-flop. In another small bowl, mix remaining 1 cup frosting with second food color to make desired color; frost top of each flip-flop. Place small candies around side edge of each flip-flop to look like jewels. Decorate top of each flip-flop with decorating icing. Cut two 6-inch pieces from fruit snack; cut pieces lengthwise in half. Arrange on flip-flops for straps. Add flowers.

1 Serving (Cake and Frosting): Calories 310 (Calories from Fat 130); Total Fat 14g (Saturated Fat 3.5g; Trans Fat 0.5g); Cholesterol 40mg; Sodium 260mg; Total Carbohydrates 43g (Dietary Fiber 0g; Sugars 30g) • % Daily Value: Vitamin A 0%; Vitamin C 0%; Calcium 6%; Iron 4% • Exchanges: 3 Other Carbohydrates, 3 Fat • Carbohydrate Choices: 3

Cutting and Assembling Flip-Flops Cake

1. Cut cake to form two flip-flop shapes.

2. On tray, arrange flip-flops.

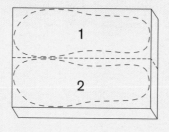

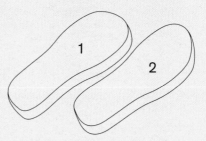

Treasure Chest Cake

1 box (1 lb 2.25 oz) chocolate fudge cake mix with pudding

Water, oil and eggs called for on cake mix box

Tray or cardboard, 24 × 20 inches, covered

Yellow and orange paste food colors

1 container (1 lb) creamy white frosting

1 tube (4.25 oz) orange decorating icing

Orange candy-coated chocolate candies

Gold foil-covered chocolate coins

Candy necklaces

Round hard candies

Gumdrop stars

Fruit stripe chewing gum

1. Heat oven to 350°F. Grease bottom only of 13 × 9–inch pan with shortening or cooking spray. In large bowl, mix cake mix, water, oil and eggs as directed on box. Pour batter into pan.

2. Bake as directed on box for 13 × 9–inch pan. Cool 10 minutes; remove from pan to wire rack. Cool completely, about 30 minutes.

3. From center of cake, cut 3-inch crosswise strip. Cut 3-inch strip diagonally in half to make two 9-inch triangular wedges. (Discard 1 cake wedge or reserve for another use.)

4. On tray, place a 9 × 5–inch cake piece. Stir food colors into frosting to make a golden yellow. Spread 1 tablespoon of frosting on 1 edge of triangular wedge of cake. Attach wedge, frosting side down, to 9 × 5–inch cake piece on tray, placing wedge along top edge of larger cake piece. Freeze all cake pieces 1 hour.

5. Spread 1 tablespoon of frosting on top edge of triangular wedge of cake. Attach remaining 9 × 5–inch cake piece to cake wedge to look like partially opened treasure chest. Spread remaining frosting over entire cake. Pull fork through frosting to look like wood grain.

6. Use decorating icing to make handles and straps. Add orange candies to handles and straps to look like studs. Fill chest with chocolate coins, candy necklaces, hard candies, gumdrop stars and gum. Add gumdrop star for clasp.

1 Serving (Cake and Frosting): Calories 420 (Calories from Fat 170); Total Fat 19g (Saturated Fat 4.5g; Trans Fat 3g); Cholesterol 55mg; Sodium 460mg; Total Carbohydrates 59g (Dietary Fiber 1g; Sugars 41g) • **% Daily Value:** Vitamin A 0%; Vitamin C 0%; Calcium 6%; Iron 10% • **Exchanges:** 1 Starch, 3 Other Carbohydrates, 3¹/₂ Fat • **Carbohydrate Choices:** 4

Personalize It! You can easily change this from a sunken treasure chest to a box full of jewels. To make a jewelry box, use bright blue or pink frosting and fill the box with lots of candy "gems" and different colors of candy necklaces.

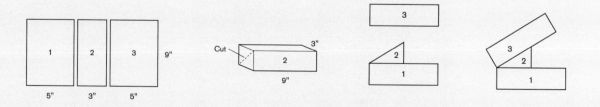

Retro Radio Cake

1 box (1 lb 2.25 oz) yellow cake mix with pudding

Water, oil and eggs called for on cake mix box

1 container (1 lb) creamy white frosting

1/2 teaspoon aqua paste or gel food color

Tray or cardboard, 20 × 15 inches, covered

Black licorice wheels

Licorice allsorts

3 strawberry rectangular sugar wafer cookies

1. Heat oven to 350°F. Grease bottom only of 13 × 9–inch pan with shortening or cooking spray. In large bowl, mix cake mix, water, oil and eggs as directed on box. Pour batter into pan.

2. Bake as directed on box for 13 × 9–inch pan. Cool 10 minutes; remove from pan to wire rack. Cool completely, about 30 minutes.

3. Cut cake crosswise into 3 equal pieces as shown in diagram. From 1 end section and the middle section, cut off domed top so pieces will be flat when stacked.

4. Reserve 1 tablespoon white frosting. Stir food color into remaining frosting to tint aqua.

5. On tray, place cake layer with flat top; spread with 1 tablespoon aqua frosting. Top with second cake piece with flat top; spread with 1 tablespoon aqua frosting. Top with remaining cake piece, placing domed top up. Freeze 1 hour.

6. Spread aqua frosting over entire stacked cake. Uncoil 2 licorice wheels; use to outline front of radio and for electrical cord. Add licorice wheel for speaker. Spread reserved white frosting in rectangle on right side of cake; add licorice allsorts for dials, buttons and on/off button. Insert cookies in top of cake for antenna; cut 1 cookie to use for cord plug.

1 Serving (Cake and Frosting): Calories 330 (Calories from Fat 140); Total Fat 15g (Saturated Fat 4.5g; Trans Fat 2.5g); Cholesterol 40mg; Sodium 310mg; Total Carbohydrates 45g (Dietary Fiber 0g; Sugars 33g) • **% Daily Value:** Vitamin A 0%; Vitamin C 0%; Calcium 6%; Iron 4% • **Exchanges:** 1 Starch, 2 Other Carbohydrates, 3 Fat • **Carbohydrate Choices:** 3

Piece of Cake! For the deepest color frosting, use paste food color.

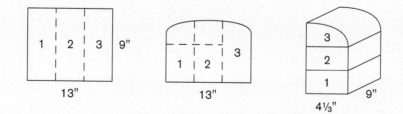

Gushing Volcano Cake

1 box (1 lb 2.25 oz) chocolate fudge
   cake mix with pudding

Water, oil and eggs called for
   on cake mix box

Tray or cardboard, 20 × 20 inches,
   covered

1 container (1 lb) milk chocolate
   creamy frosting

1 cup sugar

½ cup light corn syrup

¼ cup water

Orange and red liquid food colors

Candy rocks

1. Heat oven to 350°F. Grease 1-quart and 1½-quart ovenproof glass bowls with shortening (do not use cooking spray); coat with flour. In large mixing bowl, mix cake mix, water, oil and eggs as directed on box. Pour 1½ cups batter into 1-quart bowl and remaining batter into 1½-quart bowl.

2. Bake 1-quart bowl 40 to 45 minutes and 1½-quart bowl 45 to 50 minutes or until toothpick inserted in center comes out clean. Cool 10 minutes; remove from bowls to wire rack, placing rounded sides up. Cool completely, about 30 minutes.

3. Cut off uneven tops of cakes so they will stand flat. Place small cake with rounded side up as shown in diagram. Cut 4 evenly spaced wedges from cake, leaving 1½-inch "wall" of cake between each wedge cutout. (Discard wedges of cake or reserve for parfaits—see below.)

4. On tray, place large cake with rounded side up. Spread 1 tablespoon chocolate frosting over rounded part of large cake. Top with small cake. Freeze 1 hour.

5. To make lava, in 2-quart saucepan, heat sugar, corn syrup and water to boiling, stirring occasionally. Continue boiling, stirring occasionally, to 295°F on candy thermometer. Remove from heat; stir in 2 or 3 drops of each food color. Cool 1 to 2 minutes. Line cookie sheet with foil. Pour sugar mixture in random shapes on foil; use fork or spoon to pull through mixture to make unique "eruptions." Cool completely before removing from foil.

6. Spread chocolate frosting over entire stacked cake. Arrange lava on cake. Decorate with candy rocks.

1 Serving (Cake and Frosting): Calories 360 (Calories from Fat 130); Total Fat 15g (Saturated Fat 4g; Trans Fat 2.5g); Cholesterol 50mg; Sodium 420mg; Total Carbohydrates 55g (Dietary Fiber 0g; Sugars 38g) • % Daily Value: Vitamin A 0%; Vitamin C 0%; Calcium 4%; Iron 10% • Exchanges: 1 Starch, 2½ Other Carbohydrates, 3 Fat • Carbohydrate Choices: 3½

Personalize It! Let the kids create their parfaits from leftover cake pieces. When ready to make, just get out the goodies and layer cake pieces with yogurt, cut-up fruit, ice-cream toppings and candy sprinkles.

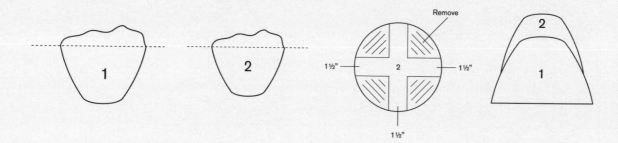

Flipped-Over Skateboard Cake

1 box (1 lb 2.25 oz) yellow cake mix with pudding

Water, oil and eggs called for on cake mix box

Tray or cardboard, 20 × 15 inches, covered

2 containers (12 oz each) fluffy white whipped frosting

Green paste food color

2 striped candy sticks

12 fudge-striped shortbread cookies

Yellow and green fruit-flavored round candies

1. Heat oven to 350°F. Grease bottom and side of 8-inch round pan with shortening or cooking spray. Grease bottom and sides of 11 × 7–inch glass baking dish with shortening (do not use cooking spray); coat with flour. In large bowl, beat cake mix, water, oil and eggs with electric mixer on low speed 30 seconds. Beat on medium speed 2 minutes, scraping bowl occasionally. Pour into pan.

2. Bake 30 to 35 minutes or until toothpick inserted in center comes out clean. Cool 10 minutes; remove from pan and baking dish to wire racks. Cool completely, about 30 minutes.

3. Cut cake as shown in diagram. Freeze pieces uncovered about 1 hour for easier frosting if desired. On tray, arrange cake pieces to form skateboard as shown in diagram; attach pieces with small amount of frosting. Stir food color into remaining frosting to tint green; frost cake.

4. Insert each end of candy sticks into 3 cookies to form axles and wheels; place on cake. Make swirls with candies on top of cake.

1 Serving (Cake and Frosting): Calories 410 (Calories from Fat 170); Total Fat 19g (Saturated Fat 4.5g; Trans Fat 0.5g); Cholesterol 40mg; Sodium 280mg; Total Carbohydrates 56g (Dietary Fiber 0g; Sugars 42g) • **% Daily Value:** Vitamin A 0%; Vitamin C 0%; Calcium 6%; Iron 4% • **Exchanges:** 1/2 Starch, 3 Other Carbohydrates, 4 Fat • **Carbohydrate Choices:** 4

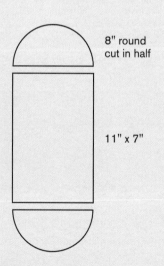

8" round cut in half

11" x 7"

Festive Holiday Cakes

Chocolate Ganache Heart Cake

1 box (1 lb 2.25 oz) chocolate fudge
cake mix with pudding

Water, oil and eggs called for
on cake mix box

1 container (1 lb) chocolate creamy
frosting

1/3 cup whipping (heavy) cream

3 oz semisweet baking chocolate,
chopped

1 bar (4 oz) white baking chocolate

Fresh edible flowers (such as violets
or pansies)

1. Heat oven to 350°F. Generously grease bottoms only of one 8-inch round pan and one 8-inch square pan with shortening.

2. Make cake mix as directed on box, using water, oil and eggs. Pour into pans.

3. Bake round and square pans 33 to 38 minutes or until toothpick inserted in center comes out clean. Cool 10 minutes; remove from pans to wire rack. Cool completely, about 1 hour.

4. Cut round cake crosswise in half. On serving plate, place square cake. Place cut sides of round cake halves against sides of square cake to form heart shape as shown in diagram; attach pieces with small amount of frosting. Spread frosting on cake.

5. To make ganache, in 1-quart saucepan, heat whipping cream over low heat until hot but not boiling; remove from heat. Stir in semisweet chocolate until melted. Let stand about 5 minutes. Ganache is ready to use when it mounds slightly when dropped from a spoon. Carefully pour ganache onto top center of cake; spread to edges, allowing some to drizzle down side.

6. Chop white chocolate bar; place in resealable food-storage plastic bag. Seal bag; microwave on High about 45 seconds or until chocolate is softened; squeeze bag until chocolate is smooth. Cut off tiny corner of bag. Drizzle white chocolate in random design around top edge of cake. Decorate cake with flowers. Store covered in refrigerator.

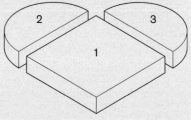

1 Serving (Cake, Frosting and Ganache): Calories 410 (Calories from Fat 200); Total Fat 22g (Saturated Fat 8g; Trans Fat 0.5g); Cholesterol 45mg; Sodium 350mg; Total Carbohydrates 49g (Dietary Fiber 1g; Sugars 36g) • **% Daily Value:** Vitamin A 2%; Vitamin C 0%; Calcium 6%; Iron 10% • **Exchanges:** 1 Starch, 2 Other Carbohydrates, 4 1/2 Fat • **Carbohydrate Choices:** 3

Design It! CHOCOLATE FLOWERS

Drizzle melted chocolate (from decorating bag or plastic bag with corner cut off) over round frosted or glazed cake, beginning with small circle in center and encircling with a larger circle 1/2 inch outside the other. Immediately draw a knife from outside edge inward and from center outward alternately 4 to 8 times to make flower design.

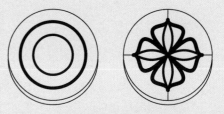

Heart and Flowers Cake

1 box (1 lb 2.25 oz) cake mix with pudding

Water, oil and eggs called for on cake mix box

1½ containers (1 lb or 12 oz each) creamy or whipped frosting (any flavor)

Assorted gumdrops

Candied orange slices, if desired

1.   Heat oven to 350°F. Grease bottoms only of one 8-inch round pan and one 8-inch square pan with shortening. Make cake mix as directed on box, using water, oil and eggs. Pour into pans.

2.   Bake as directed on box for 8-inch rounds or until toothpick inserted in center comes out clean. Cool 10 minutes; remove from pans to wire rack. Cool completely, about 1 hour.

3.   Cut round cake crosswise in half. On serving plate, place square cake. Place cut sides of round cake halves against sides of square cake to form heart shape, attaching pieces with small amount of frosting.

4.   Spread frosting on cake. On heavily sugared surface, flatten gumdrops with rolling pin until ⅛ inch thick. Cut out small petal-shaped flowers, using small cutter or knife. Pinch each flower in center to make it 3-dimensional. Cut out leaves and stems from flattened gumdrops. Arrange flowers on cake. Arrange candied orange slices to form butterfly wings and body.

1 Serving (Cake and Frosting): Calories 370 (Calories from Fat 160); Total Fat 18g (Saturated Fat 6g; Trans Fat 3.5g); Cholesterol 40mg; Sodium 320mg; Total Carbohydrates 51g (Dietary Fiber 0g; Sugars 38g) • **% Daily Value:** Vitamin A 0%; Vitamin C 0%; Calcium 6%; Iron 4% • **Exchanges:** 3½ Other Carbohydrates, 3½ Fat • **Carbohydrate Choices:** 3½

Personalize It! You can choose from many types of flowers to decorate this cake. How about Apricot Roses or Sugared Roses? See page 95 for ideas.

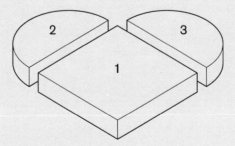

Leprechaun Village

1 box (1 lb 2.25 oz) white cake mix
  with pudding

1¼ cups water

⅓ cup vegetable oil

3 egg whites

Tray or cardboard, 18 × 16 inches,
  covered

2 containers (1 lb each) vanilla
  creamy frosting

Green liquid food color

3 sugar-style ice-cream cones
  with pointed ends

⅓ cup marshmallow bits from 1½ cups
  Lucky Charms® cereal

3 tablespoons yellow candy-coated
  fruit-flavored candies

Yellow paper baking cup, cut in half

Green decorator sugar crystals,
  if desired

Yellow decorating gel or icing
  (from 0.68- or 4.25-oz tube)

1. Heat oven to 350°F. Grease bottom only of 13 × 9–inch pan with shortening; coat with flour. In large bowl, beat cake mix, water, oil and egg whites with electric mixer on low speed 30 seconds. Beat on medium speed 2 minutes, scraping bowl occasionally. Pour into pan.

2. Bake 28 to 33 minutes or until toothpick inserted in center comes out clean. Cool 10 minutes. Run knife around sides of pan to loosen cake; remove from pan to wire rack. Cool completely, about 1 hour.

3. On tray, place cake. Spoon frosting into large bowl. Stir in 16 to 20 drops of food color until well blended. Reserve ½ cup frosting for trees; stir in 8 to 10 more drops of green food color. Frost cake with remaining frosting. Spread outside of ice-cream cones with reserved frosting. Arrange cones with pointed ends up on one corner of cake for trees. Decorate each tree with 12 to 14 marshmallow bits.

4. Arrange 2 rows of marshmallow bits from trees to within 4 inches of other short end of cake for walking path. At end of walking path, create pot of gold, using candies and baking cup. Sprinkle sugar crystals around edges of cake. Write desired message with icing or gel.

1 Serving (Cake and Frosting): Calories 450 (Calories from Fat 200); Total Fat 22g (Saturated Fat 7g; Trans Fat 5g); Cholesterol 0mg; Sodium 390mg; Total Carbohydrates 62g (Dietary Fiber 0g; Sugars 48g) • **% Daily Value:** Vitamin A 0%; Vitamin C 0%; Calcium 4%; Iron 4% • **Exchanges:** 4 Other Carbohydrates, 4½ Fat • **Carbohydrate Choices:** 4

Easter Bunny Cake

Carrot Cake (page 138)

White Mountain Frosting (page 149)

2 cups flaked or shredded coconut

Pink construction paper

Jelly beans or small gumdrops

Green liquid food color

1. Bake Carrot Cake as directed for two 8- or 9-inch rounds. Reserve 1 layer for another use. Make White Mountain Frosting. Cut 1 cake layer crosswise in half as shown in diagram. Frost top of 1 half; top with second half. On serving platter, place cake upright to form body.

2. Cut a notch about one-third of the way up one edge of body as shown in diagram. Attach cutout piece for tail with toothpicks. Frost with remaining frosting, rounding body on sides. Sprinkle with 1 cup of the coconut. Cut ears from construction paper and fold as shown in diagram; press into top. Use jelly beans for eyes and nose.

3. In resealable food-storage plastic bag, shake remaining 1 cup coconut and 3 drops food color until evenly tinted. Surround bunny with tinted coconut for grass. Add additional jelly beans.

1 Serving (Cake and Frosting): Calories 460 (Calories from Fat 230); Total Fat 25g (Saturated Fat 7g; Trans Fat 0g); Cholesterol 40mg; Sodium 230mg; Total Carbohydrates 53g (Dietary Fiber 2g; Sugars 35g) • **% Daily Value:** Vitamin A 80%; Vitamin C 0%; Calcium 2%; Iron 8% • **Exchanges:** 1½ Starch, 2 Other Carbohydrates, 5 Fat • **Carbohydrate Choices:** 3½

Time-Saver Tip: Substitute any 8- or 9-inch cake layer for the Carrot Cake. Substitute 1 box (7.2 oz) fluffy white frosting mix for the White Mountain Frosting. Make as directed on box.

Cutting and Assembling Easter Bunny Cake

1. Cut layer crosswise in half. Put halves together with frosting to form body.

2. Cut notch about one-third of the way up one edge of body to form head.

3. Attach cutout piece for tail with toothpick.

4. For ears, cut 4 × 1¾-inch pieces from pink construction paper. Fold as shown.

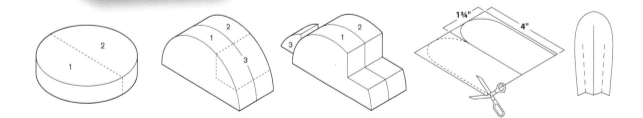

Candy-Topped Flag Cake

1. Prepare White Cake as directed for 13 × 9–inch pan—except after pouring batter into pan, randomly drop food colors over batter and cut through colors with knife for marbled design. Bake as directed.

2. Spread frosting on top and sides of cake. Place pretzel rod on top of cake for flagpole. Decorate with jelly beans to make a flag design. Write desired message on cake with decorating gel.

1 Serving (Cake and Frosting): Calories 390 (Calories from Fat 150); Total Fat 17g (Saturated Fat 5g; Trans Fat 3.5g); Cholesterol 0mg; Sodium 370mg; Total Carbohydrates 55g (Dietary Fiber 0g; Sugars 40g) • **% Daily Value:** Vitamin A 0%; Vitamin C 0%; Calcium 8%; Iron 6% • **Exchanges:** 1 Starch, 2 1/2 Other Carbohydrates, 3 1/2 Fat • **Carbohydrate Choices:** 3 1/2

White Cake (page 143)

Red and blue liquid food colors, if desired

1 container (1 lb) vanilla creamy frosting

1 pretzel rod

3/4 cup white jelly beans

3/4 cup red jelly beans

1/4 cup blue jelly beans

1 tube (0.68 oz) blue decorating gel

Firecracker Cakes

Chocolate-Cherry Cake (page 140)

Creamy Vanilla Frosting (page 146)

Red paste or gel food color

24 birthday candles

1. Bake Chocolate-Cherry Cake as directed in 24 muffin cups to make cupcakes. Make Creamy Vanilla Frosting. Remove 2 cups frosting; tint with food color.

2. Put 2 cupcakes together end-to-end with small amount of red frosting as shown in diagram. Frost sides of firecrackers with red frosting. Frost ends with white frosting. Insert a birthday candle in one end of each firecracker to look like a wick.

1 Serving (Cake and Frosting): Calories 370 (Calories from Fat 120); Total Fat 14g (Saturated Fat 6g; Trans Fat 1g); Cholesterol 35mg; Sodium 230mg; Total Carbohydrates 58g (Dietary Fiber 1g; Sugars 47g) • % Daily Value: Vitamin A 4%; Vitamin C 0%; Calcium 4%; Iron 6% • Exchanges: 1 Starch, 3 Other Carbohydrates, 2 1/2 Fat • Carbohydrate Choices: 4

Time-Saver Tip: Substitute 1 box (1 lb 2.25 oz) devil's food cake mix with pudding for the Chocolate-Cherry Cake. Bake as directed for 24 cupcakes. Substitute 2 containers (1 lb each) vanilla creamy frosting for the Creamy Vanilla Frosting.

PRESIDENTS' DAY CAKES: Make cupcakes as directed. Substitute Creamy Chocolate Frosting (page 146) for the Creamy Vanilla Frosting. Put 2 cupcakes together end-to-end with small amount of frosting. Frost sides, leaving ends unfrosted. Make strokes in frosting with fork to look like bark. Decorate with Gumdrop Hatchets.

GUMDROP HATCHETS: For each hatchet, flatten 1 large red gumdrop on heavily sugared surface with rolling pin into oval 1/8 inch thick. Cut out hatchet as shown in diagram.

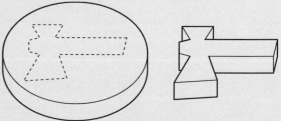

Jack-o'-Lantern Cake

Pumpkin-Gingerbread Cake (page 142)

Creamy White Frosting (page 147)

Red and yellow liquid food colors

1 green flat-bottom ice-cream cone

1 teaspoon sugar

10 large black gumdrops or 1 milk chocolate candy bar (1.55 oz)

1 tube (0.68 oz) green decorating gel

Spearmint gumdrop leaves

1. Bake Pumpkin-Gingerbread Cake as directed for two 1 1/2-quart casseroles. Make Creamy White Frosting. Tint frosting with 6 drops each red and yellow food colors to make orange.

2. Trim tops of layers to make flat if necessary. On serving plate, place 1 layer, rounded side down. Spread with 1/3 cup frosting. Place remaining layer, rounded side up, on top to make pumpkin. Frost with remaining frosting. Make vertical lines over cake with knife to shape pumpkin. Trim cone to desired height for stem; place upside down on cake.

3. On piece of waxed paper, sprinkle 1 teaspoon sugar. Place gumdrops about 1/4 inch apart on sugar. Top with another piece of waxed paper. Flatten gumdrops between waxed paper with rolling pin until 1 inch thick. Cut eyes, nose and mouth shapes from gumdrops; arrange on pumpkin for face. (Or cut candy bar into 2 large triangles for eyes and 7 small triangles for nose and mouth; arrange on pumpkin for face.) Decorate pumpkin as desired with decorating gel and spearmint gumdrops to make vines and leaves.

1 Serving (Cake and Frosting): Calories 580 (Calories from Fat 190); Total Fat 21g (Saturated Fat 8g; Trans Fat 2g); Cholesterol 90mg; Sodium 450mg; Total Carbohydrates 92g (Dietary Fiber 2g; Sugars 65g) • **% Daily Value:** Vitamin A 100%; Vitamin C 0%; Calcium 6%; Iron 15% • **Exchanges:** 1 1/2 Starch, 4 1/2 Other Carbohydrates, 4 Fat • **Carbohydrate Choices:** 6

Personalize It! Create a really frightful jack-o'-lantern by making faces on both sides of the cake. There are lots of colorful candies to choose from: candy corn, string licorice, cinnamon candies, decorating gel or piped-on chocolate or black frosting.

Time-Saver Tip: Substitute 2 containers (1 lb each) creamy white frosting for the Creamy White Frosting.

Black Cat Cake

1. Bake Dark Cocoa Cake as directed for two 8- or 9-inch rounds. Cut 1 layer as shown in diagram. Freeze cut pieces uncovered about 1 hour for easier frosting if desired. Make Creamy Cocoa Frosting. On tray, arrange uncut layer and the pieces to form cat as shown in diagram.

2. Frost cake, attaching pieces with small amount of frosting. Cut slice off bottom of each yellow gumdrop; place on cake for eyes. Use black gumdrop for nose and licorice for whiskers and lines on eyes and paws.

Dark Cocoa Cake (page 139)

Creamy Cocoa Frosting (page 146)

Tray or cardboard, 18 × 12 inches, covered

2 large yellow gumdrops

1 small black gumdrop

Black string licorice

1 Serving (Cake and Frosting): Calories 440 (Calories from Fat 160); Total Fat 18g (Saturated Fat 6g; Trans Fat 2g); Cholesterol 45mg; Sodium 320mg; Total Carbohydrates 64g (Dietary Fiber 3g; Sugars 46g) • **% Daily Value:** Vitamin A 6%; Vitamin C 0%; Calcium 2%; Iron 10% • **Exchanges:** 1 Starch, 3½ Other Carbohydrates, 3½ Fat • **Carbohydrate Choices:** 4

Cutting and Assembling Black Cat Cake

1. Cut one layer to form head, ears and tail of cat.

2. Arrange pieces around uncut layer to form cat.

Time-Saver Tip: Substitute 1 box (1 lb 2.25 oz) devil's food cake mix with pudding for the Dark Cocoa Cake. Bake as directed for two 8- or 9-inch rounds. Substitute 1½ containers (1 lb each) chocolate creamy frosting for the Creamy Cocoa Frosting.

Witches Cupcakes

1 box (1 lb 2.25 oz) yellow cake mix
    with pudding

Water, oil and eggs called for
    on cake mix box

1 container (1 lb) vanilla creamy
    frosting

Green paste food color

Black licorice twists

Candy corn

Yellow candy-coated peanut butter
    or chocolate candies

1 tube (0.68 oz) black decorating gel

1. Heat oven to 350°F. Place paper baking cup in each of 24 regular-size muffin cups. Make cake mix as directed on box, using water, oil and eggs. Fill muffin cups 2/3 full.

2. Bake 18 to 23 minutes or until toothpick inserted in center comes out clean. Immediately remove from pan to wire rack. Cool completely, about 1 hour.

3. Tint frosting with food color. Cut licorice twists into various lengths. Frost cupcakes with frosting. Arrange licorice pieces on each cupcake for hat. Add candy corn for nose and peanut butter candies for eyes. Make pupils of eyes and the mouth with decorating gel.

1 Cupcake (Cake and Frosting): Calories 210 (Calories from Fat 90); Total Fat 10g (Saturated Fat 3g; Trans Fat 1.5g); Cholesterol 25mg; Sodium 190mg; Total Carbohydrates 28g (Dietary Fiber 0g; Sugars 20g) • **% Daily Value:** Vitamin A 0%; Vitamin C 0%; Calcium 4%; Iron 2% • **Exchanges:** 2 Other Carbohydrates, 2 Fat • **Carbohydrate Choices:** 2

Black Cat Cupcakes

Dark Cocoa Cake (page 139)

Creamy Chocolate Frosting (page 146)

12 thin chocolate wafer cookies,
    cut into 4 wedges

48 red miniature jelly beans

24 blackberry nonpareil-covered
    chewy candies

Black string licorice

1. Bake Dark Cocoa Cake as directed for muffin cups to make 24 cupcakes. Make Creamy Chocolate Frosting; frost cupcakes.

2. For ears for each cupcake, add 2 wafer cookie wedges. Add red jelly beans for eyes and blackberry candy for nose. Add pieces of licorice for whiskers.

1 Cupcake (Cake and Frosting): Calories 310 (Calories from Fat 130); Total Fat 14g (Saturated Fat 6g; Trans Fat 1.5g); Cholesterol 30mg; Sodium 210mg; Total Carbohydrates 43g (Dietary Fiber 2g; Sugars 30g) • **% Daily Value:** Vitamin A 4%; Vitamin C 0%; Calcium 0%; Iron 6% • **Exchanges:** 1 Starch, 2 Other Carbohydrates, 2 1/2 Fat • **Carbohydrate Choices:** 3

Personalize It! Make Gumdrop Black Cat Cupcakes. Here's how: Bake cupcakes as directed. Make Creamy White Frosting (page 147); tint with 6 drops each red and yellow food colors to make orange. Frost cupcakes. For each gumdrop cat, cut a large black gumdrop crosswise into 3 pieces. Use small rounded top piece for head and largest bottom piece for body. Cut tail and ears from middle piece. Arrange on frosting to form cat.

Time-Saver Tip: Substitute 1 box (1 lb 2.25 oz) chocolate fudge cake mix with pudding for the Dark Cocoa Cake. Substitute 1 container (1 lb) chocolate creamy frosting for the Creamy Chocolate Frosting.

Ghost Cupcakes

White Cake (page 143)

Creamy White Frosting (page 147)

48 large marshmallows

Toothpicks

48 miniature chocolate chips

12 orange jelly beans, cut in half

1. Bake White Cake as directed for muffin cups to make 24 cupcakes. Make Creamy White Frosting; frost cupcakes, reserving some frosting for attaching ghosts.

2. For each ghost, attach 2 marshmallows with toothpick. Add chocolate chips for eyes and jelly bean half for mouth, using small amount of frosting.

3. Place ghost on each cupcake, bringing frosting up around bottom so ghost appears to be coming from frosting. Dab a small amount of frosting on top of each ghost.

1 Cupcake (Cake and Frosting): Calories 380 (Calories from Fat 120); Total Fat 13g (Saturated Fat 3.5g; Trans Fat 2g); Cholesterol 0mg; Sodium 190mg; Total Carbohydrates 64g (Dietary Fiber 0g; Sugars 51g) • **% Daily Value:** Vitamin A 0%; Vitamin C 0%; Calcium 6%; Iron 4% • **Exchanges:** 1 Starch, 3 Other Carbohydrates, 2½ Fat • **Carbohydrate Choices:** 4

Time-Saver Tip: Substitute 1 box (1 lb 2.25 oz) white cake mix with pudding for the White Cake. Substitute 2 containers (1 lb each) creamy white frosting for the Creamy White Frosting.

Turkey Gobbler Cake

1. Heat oven to 350°F. Grease bottoms only of two 9-inch round pans with shortening or cooking spray. Make cake mix as directed on box, using water, oil and eggs. Pour into pans.

2. Bake 28 to 33 minutes or until toothpick inserted in center comes out clean. Cool 10 minutes; remove from pans to wire rack. Cool completely, about 1 hour. Cut 1 layer as shown in diagram. Freeze pieces uncovered about 1 hour for easier frosting if desired.

3. On serving plate, place uncut cake round; frost top and side with frosting. Place piece 2 on frosted round; frost. Add pieces 3, 4 and 5 on piece 2 for head and feet as shown in diagram; frost.

4. Cut marshmallow in half. Moisten 1 half and dip in red sugar; join to head with frosting for turkey's wattle. Use piece from other half of marshmallow for turkey's eye. Use candy corn for beak, claws and feathers.

1 box (1 lb 2.25 oz) devil's food cake mix with pudding
Water, oil and eggs called for on cake mix box
1 container (12 oz) milk chocolate whipped frosting
1 large marshmallow
Red sugar
35 pieces candy corn

1 Serving (Cake and Frosting): Calories 300 (Calories from Fat 140); Total Fat 15g (Saturated Fat 3.5g; Trans Fat 0g); Cholesterol 40mg; Sodium 310mg; Total Carbohydrates 37g (Dietary Fiber 2g; Sugars 26g) • **% Daily Value:** Vitamin A 0%; Vitamin C 0%; Calcium 4%; Iron 10% • **Exchanges:** 1 Starch, 1½ Other Carbohydrates, 3 Fat • **Carbohydrate Choices:** 2½

Cutting and Assembling Turkey Gobbler Cake

1. Cut 1 cake round to form body, head and shoulders.

2. On plate, place uncut round; frost. Place piece 2 on top, about ½ inch from bottom edge; frost. Arrange pieces 3, 4 and 5 on piece 2.

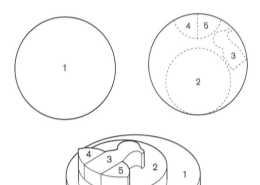

Holiday Pinecone Cake

2 cups powdered sugar

2 tablespoons meringue powder

¼ cup water

Green liquid food color

Decorating bag with tips

1½ recipes Creamy White Frosting (page 147)

2 tablespoons unsweetened baking cocoa

6 horn-shaped corn snacks

Pumpkin-Gingerbread Cake (page 142)

Tray or cardboard, 16 × 12 inches, covered

1 tube (0.68 oz) red decorating gel

1. To make pinecone needles: Draw a pair of lines, 1½ inches apart, down the length of a page of ruled paper. Make 2 more pairs of lines. Place under sheet of waxed paper. In medium bowl, beat powdered sugar, meringue powder and water with standard mixer on medium speed or with hand mixer on high speed about 2 minutes or until stiff peaks form. Tint with 3 drops green food color. (Stir in ½ teaspoon unsweetened baking cocoa if desired for a dull green color.) Place in decorating bag fitted with writing tip #5. On waxed paper, pipe 140 pine needles, 1½ inches long, inside each pair of lines, using the rules as a guide. Allow to dry at least 8 hours.

2. To make pinecones: Make Creamy White Frosting. In small bowl, mix cocoa and 1 cup frosting. Place a corn snack on waxed paper. Starting at pointed end of corn snack, pipe three petals in a circular motion with cocoa frosting and petal tip #104. Continue making petals, 1 row at a time, alternating and adding loops to shape pinecone. Finish with the bottom row, completely covering open end of corn snack. Repeat with the 5 other corn snacks. Allow to dry several hours.

3. Bake Pumpkin-Gingerbread Cake as directed for 13 × 9–inch rectangle. On tray, place cake. Reserve 1¾ cups frosting. Frost top of cake with remaining white frosting. Place 1¼ cups of the reserved frosting in decorating bag. Pipe a shell border around base of cake with star tip #5. Pipe a double shell border around top edge of cake with star tip #18.

4. Carefully remove pinecones from waxed paper and arrange on cake in upper left and lower right corners. Pipe pine branches with remaining cocoa frosting with writing tip #5. Tint remaining ½ cup frosting with 3 drops green food color. Pipe holly leaves with leaf tip #67. Pipe desired message on cake with red decorating gel. Pipe red dots for holly berries on holly leaves. Carefully remove pine needles from waxed paper and insert them around pinecones and along branches.

1 Serving (Cake and Frosting): Calories 420 (Calories from Fat 140); Total Fat 15g (Saturated Fat 8g; Trans Fat 2g); Cholesterol 57mg; Sodium 280mg; Total Carbohydrates 68g (Dietary Fiber 1g; Sugars 50g) • **% Daily Value:** Vitamin A 60%; Vitamin C 0%; Calcium 4%; Iron 10% • **Exchanges:** 1 Starch, 3 Other Carbohydrates, 3 Fat • **Carbohydrate Choices:** 4.5

Personalize It! You can use Carrot Cake (page 138) and two recipes of Cream Cheese Frosting (page 147) to make this stunning holiday cake.

Time-Saver Tip: Substitute 1 box (1 lb 2.25 oz) yellow cake mix with pudding for the Pumpkin-Gingerbread Cake. Bake as directed for 13 × 9–inch pan.

Gingerbread Cake Cottage

Pumpkin-Gingerbread Cake (page 142)

2 recipes Caramel Frosting (page 148)

Tray or cardboard, 12 × 9 inches, covered

½ recipe Creamy White Frosting
   (page 147)

Decorating bag with tips

3 multicolored striped candy sticks
   (5 inches long)

3 or 4 chocolate sugar wafer cookies

2 green licorice beans

Candy decors

4 vanilla sugar wafer cookies

1. Bake Pumpkin-Gingerbread Cake as directed for 13 × 9-inch rectangle. Cut cake as shown in diagram. Freeze pieces uncovered about 1 hour for easier frosting if desired. Make 2 recipes Caramel Frosting; remove 1½ cups. Cover remaining frosting and reserve. On tray, place cake piece 1; frost top. Frost top of piece 2; top with piece 3. Stand pieces 2 and 3 upright on piece 1 as shown in diagram. Trim corners and base so pieces fit smoothly. (Roof point will be slightly off center.) Place cake in freezer; freeze about 1 hour or until firm.

2. Make ½ recipe Creamy White Frosting. Frost exterior of house with reserved caramel frosting. Smooth frosting on front, sides and back of house with slightly dampened large metal spatula. Use the edge of a small metal spatula to press lines on front of cottage to look like logs.

3. Place about ⅓ cup vanilla frosting at a time in decorating bag fitted with writing tip #6. Break one candy stick in half. Pipe a strip of frosting down the length of each candy stick half. Press one half on each vertical front edge of house. Attach remaining candy sticks along front roof lines. Let stand about 30 minutes.

4. Cut chocolate wafer cookies to make doors and shutters. Attach with small amount of frosting piped to the back of each piece. Pipe outlines of window panes and frames. Attach licorice beans for door handles. Trim shutters with candy decors.

5. Cut vanilla wafer cookies to make chimney pieces. The back piece should be 1½ inches long, the front piece 2½ inches long. For the sides, cut two pieces each 2 inches long. Cut one end of each piece at an angle, so that the side facing the back measures 1½ inches in length and the side facing the front measures 2½ inches in length. Pipe frosting on inside vertical edges of two slanted chimney pieces. Press side pieces of chimney into frosting to form box. Hold a few minutes until set; let dry. Pipe frosting on bottom edges of chimney; place on roof.

6. Pipe any remaining frosting along roof lines, around base of chimney and around front corners of house and doors with writing tip #10 to create snowdrifts. Let stand about 30 minutes.

1 Serving (Cake and Frosting): Calories 520 (Calories from Fat 170); Total Fat 19g (Saturated Fat 9g; Trans Fat 1.5g); Cholesterol 75mg; Sodium 340mg; Total Carbohydrates 86g (Dietary Fiber 1g; Sugars 68g) • % Daily Value: Vitamin A 70%; Vitamin C 0%; Calcium 6%; Iron 10% • Exchanges: 1 Starch, 4½ Other Carbohydrates, 3½ Fat • Carbohydrate Choices: 6

Personalize It! This adorable cottage can be made out of any flavor of cake baked in a 13 × 9-inch rectangle. How about using it as a housewarming gift, decorating it to match the new house?

Cutting and Assembling Gingerbread Cake Cottage

1. Cut cake into 3 pieces.

2. On tray, place piece 1; frost top. Frost top of piece 2; top with piece 3. Stand pieces 2 and 3 upright on piece 1 to form cottage.

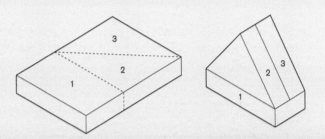

Christmas Tree Cake

White Cake (page 143)

White Mountain Frosting (page 149)

Green paste food color

Tray or cardboard, 15 × 13 inches, covered

1 chocolate flat-bottom ice-cream cone

Gumdrops

1 striped mint hard candy

1. Bake White Cake as directed for 13 × 9–inch rectangle. Cut cake as shown in diagram. Freeze pieces uncovered about 1 hour for easier frosting if desired. Make White Mountain Frosting; stir in food color.

2. On tray, arrange cake pieces 1 and 2 as shown in diagram; frost top. Trim about ½ inch from edges of top layer (piece 3); place on pieces 1 and 2. Frost sides and top of cake.

3. Insert ice-cream cone into end of tree for trunk. Cut gumdrops into ornament shapes; arrange on tree. Add striped candy to top of tree.

1 Serving (Cake and Frosting): Calories 320 (Calories from Fat 90); Total Fat 11g (Saturated Fat 3g; Trans Fat 1.5g); Cholesterol 0mg; Sodium 320mg; Total Carbohydrates 51g (Dietary Fiber 0g; Sugars 34g) • **% Daily Value:** Vitamin A 0%; Vitamin C 0%; Calcium 10%; Iron 6% • **Exchanges:** 1 Starch, 2½ Other Carbohydrates, 2 Fat • **Carbohydrate Choices:** 3½

Time-Saver Tip: Substitute 1 box (1 lb 2.25 oz) white cake mix with pudding for the White Cake. Bake as directed for 13 × 9–inch pan. Substitute 1 box (7.2 oz) fluffy white frosting mix for the White Mountain Frosting. Make as directed on box.

Cutting and Assembling Christmas Tree Cake

1. Cut cake diagonally into three pieces.

2. On tray, arrange pieces 1 and 2; frost top. Trim ½ inch from edges of piece 3. Place piece 3 on top of pieces 1 and 2.

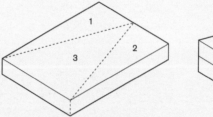 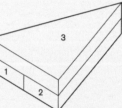

Rudolph Cupcakes

1 box (1 lb 2.25 oz) cake mix with pudding (any flavor)

Water, oil and eggs called for on cake mix box

1 container (1 lb) milk chocolate creamy frosting

24 large pretzel twists

24 blackberry nonpareil-covered chewy candies or round red candies

24 red cinnamon candies

White gumdrops

Brown miniature candy-coated chocolate baking bits

1 tube (4.25 oz) white decorating icing

1 tube (0.68 oz) black decorating gel

1. Heat oven to 350°F. Bake cake mix, using water, oil and eggs, as directed for 24 cupcakes; cool completely.

2. Spread frosting over tops of cupcakes. For each cupcake, break pretzel twist in half; arrange on cupcake for reindeer antlers.

3. Add blackberry candy or round red candy for nose. Add cinnamon candy for mouth. For eyes, cut gumdrops in half and add baking bit, using white icing to attach. Or use baking bits for eyes, adding drop of white icing and drop of black gel.

1 Cupcake (Cake and Frosting): Calories 270 (Calories from Fat 90); Total Fat 10g (Saturated Fat 3g; Trans Fat 0g); Cholesterol 25mg; Sodium 480mg; Total Carbohydrates 42g (Dietary Fiber 0g; Sugars 21g) • **% Daily Value:** Vitamin A 0%; Vitamin C 0%; Calcium 4%; Iron 8% • **Exchanges:** 1 Starch, 1½ Other Carbohydrates, 2 Fat • **Carbohydrate Choices:** 3

Personalize It! These cupcakes can easily fit into your schedule. Make ahead of time and freeze, unfrosted, in an airtight freezer container for up to four months. Then decorate the frozen cupcakes; they'll thaw while you're decorating.

Hanukkah Dreidel Cake

Hazelnut Cake (page 143)

1¹/₂ recipes Creamy White Frosting
(page 147)

Blue liquid food color

1 teaspoon unsweetened baking cocoa

Tray or cardboard, 20 × 12 inches,
covered

About ¹/₂ cup miniature chocolate chips

Decorating bag with tips

1. Bake Hazelnut Cake as directed for 13 × 9–inch rectangle. Cut cake as shown in diagram. Freeze pieces uncovered about 1 hour for easier frosting if desired. Make Creamy White Frosting. Remove 2 cups of the frosting; tint with 8 drops food color. In small bowl, mix cocoa and ¹/₄ cup of the white frosting.

2. On tray, arrange cake pieces to form dreidel as shown in diagram. Reserve ²/₃ cup white frosting; frost the center and sides of the dreidel with remaining white frosting. Reserve ²/₃ cup blue frosting; frost the dreidel point, handle top and sides with remaining blue frosting, attaching pieces with small amount of frosting. Outline the Hebrew letter of your choice with a toothpick; fill in with cocoa frosting and outline with chocolate chips.

3. Place reserved white frosting in decorating bag fitted with star tip #32; pipe a shell border along base and top edge of white-frosted cake. With reserved blue frosting, pipe a shell border along base and top edge of blue-frosted cake with shell tip. Outline top borders of white-frosted cake with chocolate chips.

1 Serving (Cake and Frosting): Calories 570 (Calories from Fat 210); Total Fat 23g (Saturated Fat 5g; Trans Fat 3.5g); Cholesterol 0mg; Sodium 300mg; Total Carbohydrates 87g (Dietary Fiber 1g; Sugars 70g) • **% Daily Value:** Vitamin A 0%; Vitamin C 0%; Calcium 10%; Iron 8% • **Exchanges:** 1¹/₂ Starch, 4¹/₂ Other Carbohydrates, 4¹/₂ Fat • **Carbohydrate Choices:** 6

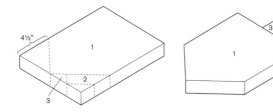

Cutting and Assembling Hanukkah Dreidel Cake

1. Cut cake to form body and handle of dreidel.

2. Arrange pieces to form dreidel.

Personalize It! Spinning the dreidel is a traditional Hanukkah game. This fun cake, made in the shape of a dreidel, will be a delightful addition to your celebration of the Jewish Festival of Lights.

Time-Saver Tip: Substitute 1 box (1 lb 2.25 oz) white cake mix with pudding for the Hazelnut Cake. Bake as directed for 13 × 9–inch pan. Substitute 2 containers (1 lb each) creamy white frosting for the Creamy White Frosting.

New Year's Cake

1. Heat oven to 350°F. Grease bottoms and sides of four 8-inch square pans with shortening or cooking spray. In large bowl, mix both cake mixes with water, oil and eggs for both mixes as directed on box. Divide batter among pans (about 2⅓ cups for each pan). Refrigerate 2 pans of batter while 2 pans bake.

2. Bake 2 pans at a time, following times on cake mix box for 8-inch round pans. Cool 10 minutes; remove from pans to wire racks. Cool completely, about 30 minutes.

3. Cut off domed top from each cake so they will be flat when stacked. On tray, place 1 cake; spread with ⅓ cup frosting. Top with second cake; spread with ⅓ cup frosting. Top with third cake; spread with ⅓ cup frosting.

4. Cut fourth cake into star shape. Place on top of stacked cakes. Freeze 1 hour.

5. In small microwavable bowl, microwave white baking chips uncovered on High 1 minute, stirring after 30 seconds, until softened; stir until smooth. Pour into decorating bag with writing tip. On piece of foil, cooking parchment paper or waxed paper, pipe stars, letters or other shapes; refrigerate until firm.

6. Spread remaining chocolate frosting over entire stacked cake. Decorate with white stars, letters and shapes.

2 boxes (1 lb 2.25 oz each) chocolate fudge cake mix with pudding

Water, oil and eggs called for on cake mix boxes

Tray or cardboard, 16 × 16 inches, covered

2 containers (1 lb each) milk chocolate creamy frosting

1 cup white vanilla baking chips

Decorating bag with tips

1 Serving (Cake and Frosting): Calories 330 (Calories from Fat 110); Total Fat 13g (Saturated Fat 4.5g; Trans Fat 2.5g); Cholesterol 20mg; Sodium 370mg; Total Carbohydrates 53g (Dietary Fiber 0g; Sugars 39g) • **% Daily Value:** Vitamin A 0%; Vitamin C 0%; Calcium 6%; Iron 10% • **Exchanges:** 1 Starch, 2½ Other Carbohydrates, 2½ Fat • **Carbohydrate Choices:** 3½

3
2
1

Celebration Cakes

Classic White Wedding Cake

6 recipes White Cake (page 143)

3 recipes Creamy White Frosting (page 147)

Large tray, mirror or foil-covered cardboard, 16 inches round

Foil-covered cardboard, 10 inches round

Foil-covered cardboard, 6 inches round

White Decorator Frosting (page 148)

Decorating bag with tips

1. Grease bottom and side of one 10 × 2–inch round pan with shortening; lightly flour. Make 1 recipe White Cake. Pour 4½ cups batter into pan. Bake 45 to 50 minutes or until top springs back when touched lightly in center. Cool 15 minutes; remove from pan. Cool completely.

2. Grease bottom and side of one 14 × 2–inch round pan and one 6 × 2–inch round pan with shortening; lightly flour. Make 2 recipes White Cake, 1 recipe at a time. Pour 1½ cups batter into 6-inch pan and 7¾ cups batter into 14-inch pan. Bake 6-inch layer 35 to 40 minutes, 14-inch layer 50 to 55 minutes, or until top springs back when touched lightly in center. Cool 15 minutes; remove from pans. Cool completely.

3. Repeat steps 1 and 2, making a total of 6 layers. Each tier of wedding cake will consist of 2 layers. (Height must measure 3 inches total, or 1½ inches per layer.) Tops of layers should be flat for ease in stacking. Slice off rounded tops if necessary.

4. Make 3 recipes Creamy White Frosting. On tray, place one 14-inch layer. Frost top with 1 cup frosting; top with remaining 14-inch layer. Frost side and top with about 3 cups frosting. Place covered 10-inch cardboard circle on first tier; place 10-inch layer on cardboard.

5. Frost top of 10-inch layer with ¾ cup frosting; top with remaining 10-inch layer. Frost side and top with 2 cups frosting. Place covered 6-inch cardboard circle on second tier; place 6-inch layer on cardboard. Frost top with ⅓ cup frosting; top with remaining 6-inch layer. Frost side and top with remaining frosting.

6. Make White Decorator Frosting, 1 recipe at a time. Place in decorating bag with petal tip #103. Make desired number of roses (see Petals, page 12); refrigerate until ready to use. Pipe shell border around top edge and base of each tier with open star tip #18. Arrange roses on cake as desired. Pipe vines with writing tip #4 and leaves with leaf tip #352 onto roses. Top with fresh flowers if desired (see Flowers, page 93).

1 Serving (Cake and Frosting): Calories 270 (Calories from Fat 90); Total Fat 10g (Saturated Fat 2.5g; Trans Fat 1.5g); Cholesterol 0mg; Sodium 230mg; Total Carbohydrates 42g (Dietary Fiber 0g; Sugars 30g) • **% Daily Value:** Vitamin A 0%; Vitamin C 0%; Calcium 8%; Iron 4% • **Exchanges:** ½ Starch, 2½ Other Carbohydrates, 2 Fat • **Carbohydrate Choices:** 3

Piece of Cake! Prepare Creamy White Frosting and White Decorator Frosting using clear vanilla to keep the frosting white. Prepare as many recipes of the decorator frosting as necessary. Prepare cake batter just before baking; measure ingredients ahead if desired. Bake cake layers the day before they are to be assembled, or bake them earlier and freeze.

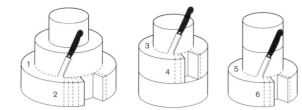

HOW TO CUT A ROUND TIERED WEDDING CAKE

You can easily cut a round, tiered wedding cake following these steps:

1.   Insert a thin, sharp or serrated knife into cake, keeping point down and handle up as shown in diagram.

2.   Slice, pulling knife toward you. If frosting sticks, dip knife in hot water or wipe with damp paper towel after cutting each slice.

3.   Cut vertically through bottom layer at edge of second layer as indicated by dotted line 1; then cut into wedges as indicated by dotted line 2.

4.   For middle layer, follow same procedure by cutting vertically through second layer at edge of top layer as indicated by dotted line 3; then cut into wedges as indicated by dotted line 4.

5.   Return to bottom layer and cut along dotted line 5; cut into wedges as indicated by dotted line 6.

6.   Separate remaining layers (traditionally, the top layer is frozen for the couple's first anniversary); cut as desired.

Apricot—Almond Wedding Cake

3 recipes Almond Cake (page 143)

2 packages (6 oz each) white chocolate baking bars

3 recipes Creamy White Frosting (page 147)

Red and yellow liquid food colors

Large tray, mirror or foil-covered cardboard, 14 inches round

1¼ cups apricot spreadable fruit

Foil-covered cardboard, 9 inches round

Chocolate Leaves (page 15)

Chocolate Twigs (page 15)

Apricot Roses (page 95)

1. Grease bottoms and sides of two 9 × 1½–inch round pans with shortening; lightly flour. Make 1 recipe Almond Cake. Divide between pans. Bake 30 to 35 minutes or until top springs back when touched lightly in center. Cool 15 minutes; remove from pans to wire rack. Cool completely.

2. Grease bottom and side of one 12 × 2–inch round pan with shortening; lightly flour. Make 1 recipe Almond Cake. Pour into pan. Bake 45 to 50 minutes or until top springs back when touched lightly in center. Cool 15 minutes; remove from pan to wire rack. Cool completely. Repeat to make second cake in 12 × 2–inch pan.

3. Each tier of wedding cake will consist of 2 layers. Tops of layers should be flat for ease in stacking. Slice off rounded tops if necessary.

4. Make white chocolate ribbons, using white chocolate baking bars, as directed for Chocolate Ribbons (page 15). Place ribbons on cookie sheet; set aside. (It is important that these be prepared before frosting the cake because they will not adhere to frosting once it is set.)

5. Make 2 recipes Creamy White Frosting. Tint with 3 drops red and 10 drops yellow food color. On tray, place one 12-inch layer. Spread ¾ cup spreadable fruit evenly over layer. Top with remaining 12-inch layer. Frost side and top. Place covered 9-inch cardboard circle on first tier.

6. Make 1 recipe Creamy White Frosting. Tint with 2 drops red and 6 drops yellow food color. Place one 9-inch layer on cardboard. Spread ½ cup spreadable fruit evenly over layer. Top with remaining layer. Frost side and top. Gently press ribbons into side and top of cake. Decorate using Apricot Roses and Chocolate Leaves and Chocolate Twigs made from white chocolate.

1 Serving (Cake and Frosting): Calories 260 (Calories from Fat 90); Total Fat 10g (Saturated Fat 2.5g; Trans Fat 1.5g); Cholesterol 0mg; Sodium 170mg; Total Carbohydrates 40g (Dietary Fiber 0g; Sugars 31g) • **% Daily Value:** Vitamin A 0%; Vitamin C 0%; Calcium 6%; Iron 4% • **Exchanges:** ½ Starch, 2 Other Carbohydrates, 2 Fat • **Carbohydrate Choices:** 2½

> **Piece of Cake!** For the entire wedding cake, prepare 3 recipes Almond Cake and 3 recipes Creamy White Frosting, using almond extract. Prepare cake batter just before baking; measure ingredients ahead if desired. Bake cake layers the day before they are to be assembled, or bake them earlier and freeze.

WEDDING CAKE YIELDS—SERVINGS PER 2-LAYER TIER

Each serving measures 2 × 1 inch from a tier 3 inches high.

LAYER	ROUND	SQUARE
6 inches	10	18
7 inches	15	–
8 inches	22	32
9 inches	28	40
10 inches	35	50
12 inches	50	72
14 inches	70	98
16 inches	100	128
18 × 12–inch rectangle		108

BAKING DIFFERENT SIZES

Layers other than sizes baked for Classic White Wedding Cake (page 90) can be made. One recipe White Cake yields about 5 cups batter.

PAN SIZE	AMOUNT OF BATTER	BAKING TIME
7 × 2–inch round	2 cups	40 to 45 minutes
8 × 2–inch round	2½ cups	40 to 45 minutes
9 × 2–inch round	3 cups	45 to 50 minutes
12 × 2–inch round	5 cups	45 to 50 minutes

Design It! FLOWERS

Add the beauty and elegance of fresh flowers to your cakes with these simple ideas:

• Select fresh flowers that can last out of water for several hours without wilting. Or insert ends of flowers in watering tubes. Good choices are buttercups, carnations, chrysanthemums, daisies, pansies, roses and violets.

• Request unsprayed flowers when ordering. If you think flowers may have been sprayed with a pesticide, dip them in soapy water, rinse thoroughly and dry before placing on cake. A small piece of plastic wrap also can be placed beneath the flowers that will touch the cake.

• Accent with baby's breath or greenery such as ferns. (See photo of Classic White Wedding Cake, page 91.)

Wedding Cupcakes

White Cake (page 143)

White paper baking cups

Creamy Vanilla Frosting (page 146)

Decorating Options

White Chocolate Curls (page 15)

Pink rose petals

Handmade paper, cut into 8 × 1¼-inch strips

Decorator sugar crystals or edible glitter

Ribbon

1. Bake White Cake as directed for muffin cups to make 24 cupcakes, using white paper baking cups. Make Creamy Vanilla Frosting; frost cupcakes.

2. Choose from these decorating options:

- Top cupcakes with White Chocolate Curls or rose petals.
- Wrap handmade paper around each cupcake; attach with permanent double-stick tape.
- Sprinkle decorator sugar crystals or edible glitter over frosting.
- Wrap ribbon around each cupcake and tie in a bow.

1 Cupcake (Cake and Frosting): Calories 320 (Calories from Fat 100); Total Fat 11g (Saturated Fat 4g; Trans Fat 1.5g); Cholesterol 15mg; Sodium 220mg; Total Carbohydrates 51g (Dietary Fiber 0g; Sugars 41g) • **% Daily Value:** Vitamin A 4%; Vitamin C 0%; Calcium 6%; Iron 4% • **Exchanges:** 3½ Other Carbohydrates, 2½ Fat • **Carbohydrate Choices:** 3½

MORE DECORATING IDEAS:

- Tint frosting to match paper colors or pick up ribbon trim colors.
- String charms on thin ribbon and anchor to paper liners with hot glue or tape.
- Cut out center of 4-inch oilproof paper doilies. Pull doily "ring" up from bottom of cupcake to just under the frosting.
- Pipe decorations with frosting (see Petals, page 12).

Time-Saver Tip: Substitute 1 box (1 lb 2.25 oz) white cake mix with pudding for the White Cake. Substitute 2 containers (1 lb each) vanilla creamy frosting for the Creamy Vanilla Frosting.

Petits Fours

White Cake (page 143)

Petits Fours Glaze (page 150)

2 cups powdered sugar

2 to 3 tablespoons water

Decorating bag with tips

1. Bake White Cake as directed for 15 × 10 × 1–inch pan. Cut cake into 1 1/2-inch squares, rounds, diamonds or hearts.

2. Make Petits Fours Glaze. Place cakes, one at a time, on wire rack over large bowl. Pour enough glaze over top to cover top and sides. (Glaze can be reheated and used again.)

3. In medium bowl, mix powdered sugar and just enough water to make a frosting that holds its shape. Place frosting in decorating bag fitted with writing tip #3. Decorate as desired.

1 Piece (Cake and Frosting): Calories 160 (Calories from Fat 25); Total Fat 2.5g (Saturated Fat 0.5g; Trans Fat 0g); Cholesterol 0mg; Sodium 85mg; Total Carbohydrates 34g (Dietary Fiber 0g; Sugars 28g) • **% Daily Value:** Vitamin A 0%; Vitamin C 0%; Calcium 2%; Iron 0% • **Exchanges:** 2 Other Carbohydrates, 1/2 Fat • **Carbohydrate Choices:** 2

Time-Saver Tip: Substitute 1 box (1 lb 2.25 oz) white cake mix with pudding. Prepare as directed on box–except bake as directed in White Cake recipe for 15 × 10 × 1–inch pan.

CAKES IN BLOOM

With the right ingredients, you can easily create beautiful flower garnishes for your cakes in minutes.

Apricot Rose: Roll 4 large dry apricot halves on well-sugared surface into ovals 1/8 inch thick. Sprinkle with sugar. Cut ovals in half. Roll 1 half-oval tightly to form center of rose. Place more half-ovals around center, overlapping slightly. Press together at base; trim base. Roll out green gumdrops to cut leaves if desired.

Marshmallow Flowers: Spray fingers and kitchen scissors with cooking spray to keep marshmallows from sticking. To make 3 flowers, snip tops of 3 pink miniature marshmallows into thirds, using kitchen scissors, without cutting entirely through marshmallows. Fan pink marshmallow pieces out. Snip 1 green miniature marshmallow into 3 pieces; flatten pieces slightly. Attach 1 green piece for leaf under each pink flower by pressing gently in place. Press a silver nonpareil in center of each flower. Remove nonpareils before eating flowers.

Sugared Roses: Dip small fresh roses in water, rinse and pat dry. Trim stems to about 2 inches. Mix 2 tablespoons light corn syrup and 1 teaspoon water. Brush mixture on rose petals with small, soft brush, separating petals as you coat them. Sift or sprinkle superfine or granulated sugar lightly on roses, shaking gently to remove excess sugar. Other flowers that can be sugared are bachelor buttons, carnations, chrysanthemums, small orchids, sweet peas and violets. Do not eat flowers.

Whipped Cream Rosettes: In chilled medium bowl, beat 1 cup whipping (heavy) cream and 2 tablespoons powdered sugar with electric mixer on high speed until stiff peaks form. Fill decorating bag. Pipe rosettes (see How to Make Rosettes, page 12) onto waxed paper–lined cookie sheet. Freeze until firm; carefully remove from waxed paper. Wrap and store in freezer. Use to decorate cakes that will be cut and served, or place on individual serving as they are cut.

Anniversary Cake

Pastel Marble Cake (page 143)

Buttercream Frosting (page 145)

Yellow liquid food color

Decorating bag with tips

Fresh flower decorations (see page 93),
if desired

1. Bake Pastel Marble Cake as directed for 13 × 9–inch rectangle. Make Buttercream Frosting; stir in 3 or 4 drops food color. Reserve half of the frosting for decorating. Frost cake with remaining frosting.

2. Place half of the reserved frosting at a time in decorating bag fitted with writing tip. Pipe scalloped outline in center of cake, and add dots to top of cake outside scalloped outline in dotted Swiss pattern. With star tip #18, pipe shell borders around top and bottom edges of cake. Pipe message in center of cake. Decorate with flower decorations.

1 Serving (Cake and Frosting): Calories 500 (Calories from Fat 200); Total Fat 23g (Saturated Fat 7g; Trans Fat 3g); Cholesterol 20mg; Sodium 340mg; Total Carbohydrates 70g (Dietary Fiber 0g; Sugars 54g) • **% Daily Value:** Vitamin A 6%; Vitamin C 0%; Calcium 10%; Iron 6% • **Exchanges:** 1 Starch, 3$\frac{1}{2}$ Other Carbohydrates, 4$\frac{1}{2}$ Fat • **Carbohydrate Choices:** 4$\frac{1}{2}$

Piece of Cake! This pretty and unusual cake will also be perfect for showers and birthdays or as a small wedding cake.

Time-Saver Tip: Substitute 1 box (1 lb 2.25 oz) white cake mix with pudding for the Pastel Marble Cake. Bake as directed for 13 × 9–inch pan–except tint batter and spoon into pan as directed in the Pastel Marble Cake recipe.

Baby Bib Shower Cake

Hazelnut Cake (page 143)

Creamy Vanilla Frosting (page 146)

Decorating bag with tips

Blue and red liquid food colors

Green and yellow liquid food colors,
    if desired

Small candy mints

1. Bake Hazelnut Cake as directed for two 8- or 9-inch rounds. Make Creamy Vanilla Frosting; reserve 1 cup. Fill layers and frost side and top of cake with remaining frosting. Make tines of fork on side of cake or horizontal lines with decorating comb if desired.

2. Place 1/2 cup of the reserved frosting in decorating bag with round tip. Pipe zigzag border around outer top edge of cake.

3. Tint 1/4 cup of the reserved frosting with blue food color and place in decorating bag fitted with writing tip. Pipe outer border of bib with blue frosting. Pipe inner opening of bib about 3 inches in diameter; join circles with tie at top. Write desired message in bib opening with blue frosting. Tint 1/4 cup of the reserved frosting with red food color to make pink. Pipe dots and ribbons on bib with small round tip. Arrange mints around base of cake.

1 Serving (Cake and Frosting): Calories 540 (Calories from Fat 190); Total Fat 21g (Saturated Fat 7g; Trans Fat 2g); Cholesterol 25mg; Sodium 360mg; Total Carbohydrates 83g (Dietary Fiber 1g; Sugars 66g) • **% Daily Value:** Vitamin A 8%; Vitamin C 0%; Calcium 10%; Iron 8% • **Exchanges:** 1 Starch, 4 1/2 Other Carbohydrates, 4 Fat • **Carbohydrate Choices:** 5 1/2

Time-Saver Tip: Substitute 1 box (1 lb 2.25 oz) white cake mix with pudding for the Hazelnut Cake. Bake as directed for two 8- or 9-inch rounds. Substitute 2 containers (1 lb each) vanilla creamy frosting for the Creamy Vanilla Frosting.

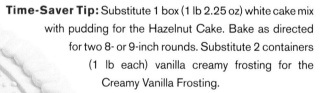

Bootie Shower Cakes

1. Bake White Cake as directed for 24 regular-size muffin cups to make cupcakes. Remove paper baking cups if used. Place 2 cupcakes upside down on separate plates. Cut small piece off side of a third cupcake to form flat surface. Cut third cupcake horizontally in half. Place one half with cut side against cupcake on plate to form bootie as shown in diagram. Place remaining half against second cupcake. Repeat with remaining cupcakes.

> **White Cake (page 143)**
> **White Mountain Frosting (page 149)**
> **Food colors, if desired**
> **Decorating bag with tips**
> **Striped fruit-flavored gum**

2. Make White Mountain Frosting; reserve ⅔ cup. Tint remaining frosting with food color if desired. Frost booties, attaching pieces with small amount of frosting. Place reserved frosting in decorating bag fitted with writing tip #4. Outline top and tongue of booties with frosting. Cut gum into strips for accents and lace; place on booties.

1 Bootie (Cake and Frosting): Calories 280 (Calories from Fat 80); Total Fat 9g (Saturated Fat 2.5g; Trans Fat 1.5g); Cholesterol 0mg; Sodium 290mg; Total Carbohydrates 46g (Dietary Fiber 0g; Sugars 30g) • **% Daily Value:** Vitamin A 0%; Vitamin C 0%; Calcium 8%; Iron 6% • **Exchanges:** 1 Starch, 2 Other Carbohydrates, 2 Fat • **Carbohydrate Choices:** 3

Personalize It! For a traditional look, tint the booties pastel yellow, blue or pink. For a fun, contemporary look, use bright primary colors.

Time-Saver Tip: Substitute 1 box (1 lb 2.25 oz) white cake mix with pudding for the White Cake. Bake as directed for 24 cupcakes. Substitute 2 boxes (7.2 oz each) fluffy white frosting mix for the White Mountain Frosting. Make as directed on box.

Cutting and Assembling Bootie Shower Cakes

1. Cut piece off side of one cupcake.

2. Cut cupcake horizontally in half.

3. Place halves with cut sides against two other cupcakes.

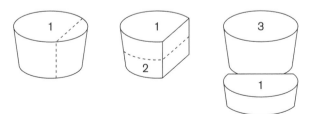

Almond Baby Cakes

1 box (1 lb 2.25 oz) white cake mix
    with pudding

1¼ cups water

⅓ cup vegetable oil

1 teaspoon almond extract

3 egg whites

Petits Fours Glaze (page 150)

Assorted colors decorating icing
    (in 4.25-oz tubes)

1. Heat oven to 375°F. Grease bottoms only of about 60 mini muffin cups with shortening or cooking spray. In large bowl, beat cake mix, water, oil, almond extract and egg whites with electric mixer on low speed 30 seconds. Beat on medium speed 2 minutes, scraping bowl occasionally. Divide batter evenly among muffin cups (about ½ full). (If using one pan, refrigerate batter while baking other cakes; wash pan before filling with additional batter.)

2. Bake 10 to 15 minutes or until toothpick inserted in center comes out clean. Cool 5 minutes; remove from pan to wire rack. Cool completely, about 30 minutes.

3. Make Petits Fours Glaze. Place wire rack on cookie sheet or waxed paper to catch glaze drips. Turn each baby cake on wire rack so top side is down. Pour about 1 tablespoon glaze over each baby cake, letting glaze coat the sides. Let stand 15 minutes.

4. With decorating icing, pipe designs on cakes in shapes of letters, animals, safety pins, booties, rattles or bottles. You can bake the baby cakes up to 2 weeks ahead of time. Freeze, then add the glaze right before the party.

1 Baby Cake (Cake and Frosting): Calories 120 (Calories from Fat 20); Total Fat 2g (Saturated Fat 0g; Trans Fat 0g); Cholesterol 0mg; Sodium 65mg; Total Carbohydrates 24g (Dietary Fiber 0g; Sugars 21g) • **% Daily Value:** Vitamin A 0%; Vitamin C 0%; Calcium 0%; Iron 0% • **Exchanges:** ½ Starch, 1 Other Carbohydrates, ½ Fat • **Carbohydrate Choices:** 1½

Personalize It! Baby cakes are great for themed parties, too, like an anniversary or going away party. Pipe one individual letter on each cake to spell out "Best Wishes" or "Bon Voyage."

Happy Birthday Cell Phone Cake

1 box (1 lb 2.25 oz) white cake mix with pudding

Water, oil and egg whites called for on cake mix box

Tray or cardboard, 18 × 16 inches, covered

1½ containers (1 lb each) creamy white frosting

Pink paste or gel food color

Decorating bag with tips

12 white candy-coated chewing gum squares

1 package (3.2 oz) marshmallow flowers

3 oval licorice candies

1 candy straw

1. Heat oven to 350°F. Grease bottom only of 13 × 9–inch pan with shortening or cooking spray. In large bowl, mix cake mix, water, oil and egg whites as directed on box. Pour batter into pan.

2. Bake as directed on box for 13 × 9–inch pan. Cool 10 minutes; remove from pan to wire rack. Cool completely, about 30 minutes.

3. Cut 1¼-inch strip from each long side of cake. Trim each corner of cake to round off, making cell phone shape. (Discard pieces trimmed from cake or reserve for another use.) On tray, place cake. Freeze 1 hour.

4. Divide 1 container of white frosting in half (about ¾ cup each). Stir food color into half of frosting to tint pink. Spread pink frosting over bottom two-thirds of cake. Spread white frosting over top one-third of cake.

5. From ½ container of frosting, reserve about 2 tablespoons white frosting. Tint about ¼ cup of the frosting pink. Onto center of white-frosted third of cake, spread some of the pink frosting in square shape for message screen. Place remaining pink frosting in decorating bag fitted with writing tip. Pipe pink frosting along edge of white-frosted cake. Arrange gum on cake for number buttons; pipe on numbers with pink frosting.

6. With reserved white frosting, pipe desired message on message screen. Add marshmallow flowers and licorice candies. Add candy straw for antenna.

1 Serving (Cake and Frosting): Calories 390 (Calories from Fat 160); Total Fat 18g (Saturated Fat 6g; Trans Fat 4g); Cholesterol 0mg; Sodium 350mg; Total Carbohydrates 53g (Dietary Fiber 0g; Sugars 40g) • **% Daily Value:** Vitamin A 0%; Vitamin C 0%; Calcium 4%; Iron 4% • **Exchanges:** 1 Starch, 2½ Other Carbohydrates, 3½ Fat • **Carbohydrate Choices:** 3½

Personalize It! You can write any message you want on this colorful cake. You will get the most vivid color from paste or gel food color, but if you have only liquid food color, use about 10 drops to make the frosting bright red.

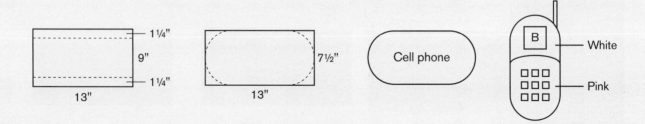

Poppin' Up Happy Birthday Cake

1 box (1 lb 2.25 oz) yellow cake mix
with pudding

Water, oil and eggs called for
on cake mix box

1 container (1 lb) creamy white frosting

Tray or cardboard, 24 × 16 inches,
covered

Red pull-and-peel licorice

¼ bar (4-oz size) white chocolate

1 tube (4.25 oz) blue decorating icing

2 cups popped kettle corn

1. Heat oven to 350°F. Grease bottom and side of 8-inch round pan with shortening or cooking spray. Grease bottom and sides of 11 × 7–inch glass baking dish with shortening (do not use cooking spray); coat with flour. In large bowl, mix cake mix, water, oil and eggs as directed on box. Pour 1½ cups batter into 8-inch round pan and remaining batter into 11 × 7–inch baking dish.

2. Bake 30 to 35 minutes or until toothpick inserted in center comes out clean. Cool 10 minutes; remove from pan and baking dish to wire racks. Cool completely, about 30 minutes.

3. Cut 8-inch round cake crosswise in half. Spread 1 tablespoon frosting over top of 1 cake piece. Top with second cake piece.

4. Cut wedge shape from each long side of 11 × 7–inch cake, so cake is 4 inches wide at one end and 7 inches wide at other end. On tray, place larger cake piece with 4-inch end at one end of tray. Using 2 tablespoons frosting to attach pieces, arrange wedge-shaped pieces on 7-inch end of larger cake as shown in diagram. Cut off pointed ends that hang over side of cake; arrange ends on cake as shown in diagram. This cake is the popcorn bag.

5. Place stacked rounded cake at 7-inch end of cake on tray. This cake is the kettle corn. Freeze 1 hour.

6. Spread remaining frosting over entire cake. Peel 5 sections of licorice apart; arrange lengthwise on popcorn bag.

7. Place white chocolate bar on center of popcorn bag. Write "Happy Birthday" on bar with decorating icing.

8. Press kettle corn onto top of cake.

1 Serving (Cake and Frosting): Calories 330 (Calories from Fat 140); Total Fat 15g (Saturated Fat 4.5g; Trans Fat 2.5g); Cholesterol 40mg; Sodium 310mg; Total Carbohydrates 45g (Dietary Fiber 0g; Sugars 33g) • **% Daily Value:** Vitamin A 0%; Vitamin C 0%; Calcium 6%; Iron 4% • **Exchanges:** 1 Starch, 2 Other Carbohydrates, 3 Fat • **Carbohydrate Choices:** 3

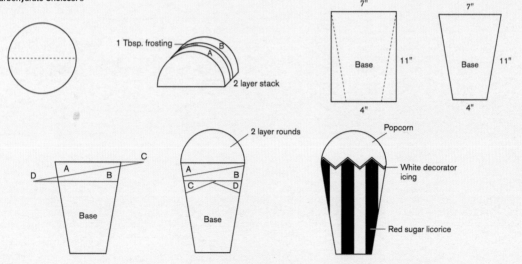

Mother's Day Hat Cake

1 box (1 lb 2.25 oz) cake mix with pudding

Water, oil and eggs called for on cake mix box

2 containers (1 lb or 12 oz each) creamy or whipped frosting

Clean wicker basket

Ribbon and edible flowers (such as dianthus, pansies, violas)

1. Heat oven to 350°F. Grease bottoms only of one 8-inch round pan and one 9-inch round pan with shortening. Make cake mix as directed on box, using water, oil and eggs. Pour into pans.

2. Bake as directed on box or until toothpick inserted in center comes out clean. Cool 10 minutes; remove from pans to wire rack. Cool completely, about 1 hour.

3. Cut 6-inch circle out of waxed paper; place on 8-inch round. Cut cake around circle with small knife to make 6-inch round layer. Place on 9-inch round, attaching pieces with small amount of frosting.

4. Frost cake. Add texture to frosting by gently rolling wicker basket over frosting. Trim hat with ribbon and flowers.

1 Serving (Cake and Frosting): Calories 430 (Calories from Fat 190); Total Fat 22g (Saturated Fat 7g; Trans Fat 0.5g); Cholesterol 40mg; Sodium 380mg; Total Carbohydrates 57g (Dietary Fiber 0g; Sugars 41g) • **% Daily Value:** Vitamin A 0%; Vitamin C 0%; Calcium 6%; Iron 10% • **Exchanges:** 4 Other Carbohydrates, 4½ Fat • **Carbohydrate Choices:** 4

Gone Fishin' Cake

1. Bake Buttermilk Spice Cake as directed for 15 × 10 × 1–inch pan. Place on tray. Make Creamy Vanilla Frosting; reserve ⅔ cup. Frost cake with remaining frosting, making top smooth. Place 1 drop food color on tip of spatula. Pat color in several places along bottom of cake; swirl into frosting for water.

2. Sift cocoa over reserved frosting; stir until smooth, adding 1 to 2 teaspoons water if necessary. Place cocoa frosting in decorating bag fitted with writing tip #2. Write desired "Gone Fishing" message on cake. Place candy stick and ring-shaped hard candy on top of cake to form fishing rod and reel. Pipe on fishing line with cocoa frosting. Place gummy frog or fish at end of fishing line for bait.

3. Pipe stringer on cake with cocoa frosting. Arrange gummy fish around stringer. Pipe shell border around top edge and base of cake with cocoa frosting and star tip #18.

Buttermilk Spice Cake (page 138)

Tray or cardboard, 18 × 13 inches, covered

Creamy Vanilla Frosting (page 146)

Blue liquid food color

¼ cup unsweetened baking cocoa

Decorating bag with tips

1 striped candy stick (5 inches long)

1 ring-shaped hard candy

1 gummy frog or fish-shaped candy

3 to 5 gummy fish candies

1 Serving (Cake and Frosting): Calories 430 (Calories from Fat 130); Total Fat 14g (Saturated Fat 6g; Trans Fat 1.5g); Cholesterol 55mg; Sodium 310mg; Total Carbohydrates 72g (Dietary Fiber 1g; Sugars 57g) • **% Daily Value:** Vitamin A 6%; Vitamin C 0%; Calcium 6%; Iron 8% • **Exchanges:** 1 Starch, 4 Other Carbohydrates, 2½ Fat • **Carbohydrate Choices:** 5

Personalize It! Use colorful candies, fruit snacks and even real fishing lures to personalize this cake for a fishing enthusiast.

Father's Day Hawaiian Shirt Cake

Hazelnut Cake (page 143)

Creamy White Frosting (page 147)

Blue paste food color

Tray or cardboard, 16 × 14 inches, covered

Fruit-shaped candies

Small pretzel sticks

Spearmint gumdrop leaves, cut horizontally in half

1. Bake Hazelnut Cake as directed for 13 × 9–inch rectangle. Cut cake as shown in diagram. Freeze the main piece uncovered about 1 hour for easier frosting if desired.

2. Make Creamy White Frosting; stir in food color to make light blue. Remove 1/2 cup frosting; stir in additional food color to make darker blue.

3. Arrange cake on tray. Frost with light blue frosting. Spread darker blue frosting randomly into light blue frosting.

4. Decorate with fruit candies, using orange candies for buttons. Make palm trees with pretzel sticks and gumdrop leaves.

1 Serving (Cake and Frosting): Calories 480 (Calories from Fat 180); Total Fat 20g (Saturated Fat 4.5g; Trans Fat 2.5g); Cholesterol 0mg; Sodium 300mg; Total Carbohydrates 71g (Dietary Fiber 1g; Sugars 55g) • **% Daily Value:** Vitamin A 0%; Vitamin C 0%; Calcium 10%; Iron 8% • **Exchanges:** 1 Starch, 4 Other Carbohydrates, 4 Fat • **Carbohydrate Choices:** 5

Cutting and Assembling Father's Day Hawaiian Shirt Cake

Cut cake to form shirt and sleeves.

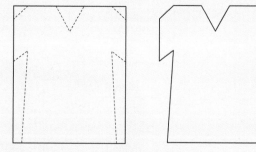

Time-Saver Tip: Substitute 1 box (1 lb 2.25 oz) white cake mix with pudding for the Hazelnut Cake. Bake as directed for 13 × 9–inch pan. Substitute 2 containers (1 lb each) creamy white frosting for the Creamy White Frosting.

Housewarming Cake

Whole Wheat Applesauce Cake
(page 137)

Tray or cardboard, 16 × 12 inches,
covered

Creamy Vanilla Frosting (page 146)

Black string licorice

Vanilla sugar wafer cookies

Green candy sprinkles

Lemon candied fruit slice

3 oval licorice candies

1/2 large orange gumdrop

Green rock candy

Yellow liquid food color

Decorating bag with tips

1 tube (0.68 oz) black decorating gel

1. Bake Whole Wheat Applesauce Cake as directed for 13 × 9–inch rectangle. Place on tray. Make Creamy Vanilla Frosting; reserve 2 tablespoons. Frost cake with remaining frosting. Outline door and make bricks with a toothpick or knife.

2. Outline door frame with string licorice. Attach wafer cookies at base of door for stoop. Use green sprinkles for grass, fruit slice for window, oval licorice candies for hinges and door handle, gumdrop for planter and rock candy for plant. Add flowers as desired.

3. Tint reserved frosting with 5 drops of food color. Place in decorating bag fitted with writing tip #4. Pipe on house number and mailbox. Write new neighbor's name with decorating gel.

1 Serving (Cake and Frosting): Calories 530 (Calories from Fat 170); Total Fat 19g (Saturated Fat 6g; Trans Fat 1.5g); Cholesterol 50mg; Sodium 440mg; Total Carbohydrates 86g (Dietary Fiber 3g; Sugars 67g) • **% Daily Value:** Vitamin A 8%; Vitamin C 0%; Calcium 4%; Iron 8% • **Exchanges:** 1 Starch, 4 1/2 Other Carbohydrates, 4 Fat • **Carbohydrate Choices:** 6

Time-Saver Tip: Substitute 1 box (1 lb 2.25 oz) yellow or spice cake mix with pudding for the Whole Wheat Applesauce Cake. Bake as directed for 13 × 9–inch pan.

Star of David Cake

1. Bake White Cake as directed for 13 × 9–inch rectangle. Cut cake as shown in diagram. Freeze pieces uncovered about 1 hour for easier frosting if desired. Make Creamy White Frosting; reserve 1½ cups.

2. On tray, arrange cake pieces to form star as shown in diagram, attaching pieces with small amount of frosting. Frost cake with remaining white frosting. Place ½ cup of the reserved frosting in decorating bag with star tip #32. Pipe shell border around base of cake. Tint remaining reserved frosting with desired food color. Pipe 3 rows of stars with star tip #32 around top edge of cake, starting and stopping so that triangles appear interwoven. Sprinkle colored sugar lightly over white frosting; sprinkle on border if desired.

> **White Cake (page 143)**
>
> **Creamy White Frosting (page 147)**
>
> **Tray or cardboard, 14 × 14 inches, covered**
>
> **Decorating bag with tips**
>
> **Food color (in desired color)**
>
> **Colored sugar**

1 Serving (Cake and Frosting): Calories 440 (Calories from Fat 150); Total Fat 17g (Saturated Fat 4g; Trans Fat 2.5g); Cholesterol 0mg; Sodium 300mg; Total Carbohydrates 70g (Dietary Fiber 0g; Sugars 54g) • **% Daily Value:** Vitamin A 0%; Vitamin C 0%; Calcium 10%; Iron 6% • **Exchanges:** 1 Starch, 3½ Other Carbohydrates, 3½ Fat • **Carbohydrate Choices:** 4½

Time-Saver Tip: Substitute 1 box (1 lb 2.25 oz) white cake mix with pudding for the White Cake. Bake as directed for 13 × 9–inch pan. Substitute 2 containers (1 lb each) creamy white frosting for the Creamy White Frosting.

Cutting and Assembling Star of David Cake

1. Cut cake to form one large triangle and three smaller ones.

2. Arrange smaller triangles around large triangle to complete star points.

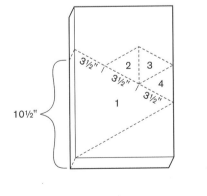

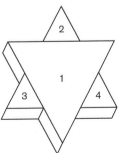

Decorated Cupcakes

Snowman Cupcakes

White Cake (page 143)

Creamy Vanilla Frosting (page 146)

White edible glitter or decorator sugar crystals

1 bag (16 oz) large marshmallows

Pretzel sticks

Chewy fruit snack in 3-foot rolls, any red or orange flavor (from 4.5-oz box)

Assorted candies (such as gumdrops, gummy ring candies, peppermint candies, chocolate chips, pastel mint chips, candy decors, string licorice)

1. Bake White Cake as directed for muffin cups to make 24 cupcakes. Make Creamy Vanilla Frosting; frost cupcakes. Sprinkle frosting with edible glitter.

2. Stack 2 or 3 marshmallows on each cupcake, using 1/2 teaspoon frosting between marshmallows to attach.

3. For arms, break pretzel sticks into pieces 1 1/2 inches long. Press 2 pieces into marshmallow on each cupcake. Cut 1-inch mitten shapes from fruit snack. Attach mittens to pretzels.

4. For scarf, cut fruit snack into 6 × 1/4–inch piece; wrap and tie around base of top marshmallow. For hat, stack candies, using frosting to attach. For earmuff, use piece of string licorice and candies, using frosting to attach.

5. For faces and buttons, attach desired candies with small amount of frosting.

1 Cupcake (Cake and Frosting): Calories 390 (Calories from Fat 100); Total Fat 11g (Saturated Fat 4g; Trans Fat 1.5g); Cholesterol 15mg; Sodium 230mg; Total Carbohydrates 69g (Dietary Fiber 0g; Sugars 53g) • % Daily Value: Vitamin A 4%; Vitamin C 0%; Calcium 6%; Iron 4% • Exchanges: 1 Starch, 3 1/2 Other Carbohydrates, 2 Fat • Carbohydrate Choices: 4 1/2

Time-Saver Tip: Substitute 1 box (1 lb 2.25 oz) white cake mix with pudding for the White Cake. Substitute 1 1/2 containers (1 lb each) creamy vanilla frosting for the Creamy Vanilla Frosting.

Personalize It! There are lots of clever ways that snow people can be decorated; check your pantry for colorful candies you might have on hand and make your own snow creatures!

Ball Game Cupcakes

1 box (1 lb 2.25 oz) yellow cake mix with pudding

1 cup water

1/3 cup vegetable oil

3 large eggs

1 cup miniature semisweet chocolate chips

1 container (1 lb) vanilla creamy frosting

Assorted colors decorating icing (in 4.25-oz tubes)

Assorted food colors

1. Heat oven to 375°F. Place paper baking cup in each of 24 regular-size muffin cups. In large bowl, beat cake mix, water, oil and eggs with electric mixer on low speed 30 seconds. Beat on medium speed 2 minutes, scraping bowl occasionally. Fold in chocolate chips. Divide batter evenly among muffin cups (2/3 full).

2. Bake 20 to 25 minutes or until toothpick inserted in center comes out clean. Cool 10 minutes; remove from pan to wire rack. Cool completely, about 30 minutes.

3. For soccer balls, frost cupcakes with vanilla frosting. With black icing, pipe a pentagon shape in the center of cupcake, piping a few rows of icing into center of pentagon. Using a toothpick, trace a line from each point of pentagon to edge of cupcake to look like seams. With toothpick or spatula, spread black icing in center of pentagon to fill in the entire shape.

4. For baseballs, frost cupcakes with vanilla frosting. With red, black or blue icing, pipe 2 arches on opposite sides of cupcakes, curving lines slightly toward center. Pipe small lines from each arch to look like stitches on a baseball.

5. For basketballs, tint frosting with yellow and red food colors to make orange; frost cupcakes. With black icing, pipe line across center of cupcake. On either side, pipe an arch that curves slightly toward center line, then pipe a short line from center of each arch to edge of cupcake.

6. For tennis balls, tint frosting with yellow and green food colors to make tennis-ball yellow; frost cupcakes. With white icing, pipe curved design to look like tennis balls.

1 Cupcake (Cake and Frosting): Calories 250 (Calories from Fat 110); Total Fat 12g (Saturated Fat 4g; Trans Fat 2g); Cholesterol 25mg; Sodium 200mg; Total Carbohydrates 33g (Dietary Fiber 0g; Sugars 25g) • % Daily Value: Vitamin A 0%; Vitamin C 0%; Calcium 4%; Iron 4% • Exchanges: 2 Other Carbohydrates, 2 1/2 Fat • Carbohydrate Choices: 2

Personalize It! Go for extra smiles from your sports fans: arrange baseball cupcakes on a clean baseball base; line a tray with artificial grass for soccer ball cupcakes; or surround a platter of basketball or tennis ball cupcakes with a net.

Happy Birthday Marshmallow Cupcakes

White Cake (page 143)

Creamy Vanilla Frosting (page 146)

24 to 30 large marshmallows

Colored sugar or candy sprinkles

White or colored birthday candles

1. Bake White Cake as directed for muffin cups to make 24 cupcakes. Make Creamy Vanilla Frosting; frost cupcakes.

2. Cut marshmallow with dampened kitchen scissors into slices; sprinkle with colored sugar. Arrange on cupcakes in flower shape. Place candle in middle of each flower.

1 Cupcake (Cake and Frosting): Calories 360 (Calories from Fat 110); Total Fat 12g (Saturated Fat 4.5g; Trans Fat 1.5g); Cholesterol 15mg; Sodium 240mg; Total Carbohydrates 61g (Dietary Fiber 0g; Sugars 50g) • % **Daily Value:** Vitamin A 4%; Vitamin C 0%; Calcium 6%; Iron 4% • **Exchanges:** 1 Starch, 3 Other Carbohydrates, 2 Fat • **Carbohydrate Choices:** 4

Time-Saver Tip: Substitute 1 box (1 lb 2.25 oz) white cake mix with pudding for the White Cake. Substitute 2 containers (1 lb each) vanilla creamy frosting for the Creamy Vanilla Frosting.

Personalize It! Make Marshmallow Flower Cupcakes: Prepare as directed above except insert round colored candy in center instead of candle.

Lion Cupcakes

SEE PHOTO ON PAGE 113 • **24 CUPCAKES**

Yellow Cake (page 144)

Creamy Vanilla Frosting (page 146)
or Creamy Chocolate Frosting
(page 146)

Yellow paste or gel food color

Assorted candies (such as candy-
coated chocolate candies, pastel
mint chips, gumdrops, jelly beans)

1 tube (4.25 oz) chocolate or white
decorating icing

3 cups chow mein noodles

1. Bake Yellow Cake as directed for muffin cups to make 24 cup-cakes. Make Creamy Vanilla Frosting; tint with food color to make yellow. (Or make Creamy Chocolate Frosting.) Frost cupcakes.

2. Add candies for ears, eyes and muzzles. Pipe on whiskers with decorating icing. Add noodles along edge of each cupcake for mane.

1 Cupcake (Cake and Frosting): Calories 330 (Calories from Fat 90); Total Fat 10g (Saturated Fat 5g; Trans Fat 0.5g); Cholesterol 50mg; Sodium 250mg; Total Carbohydrates 57g (Dietary Fiber 0g; Sugars 46g) • % Daily Value: Vitamin A 8%; Vitamin C 0%; Calcium 6%; Iron 4% • Exchanges: 1 Starch, 3 Other Carbohydrates, 2 Fat • Carbohydrate Choices: 4

Time-Saver Tip: Substitute 1 box (1 lb 2.25 oz) yellow cake mix with pudding for the Yellow Cake. Substitute 2 containers (1 lb each) vanilla creamy frosting for the Creamy Vanilla Frosting.

Clown Cupcakes

SEE PHOTO ON PAGE 113 • **24 CUPCAKES**

Yellow Cake (page 144)

Creamy Vanilla Frosting (page 146)

Assorted candies (such as chewy fruit-
flavored candy drops and miniature
candy-coated chocolate baking bits)

Candy coating wafers

Nonpareil decors

1 tube (4.25 oz) red decorating icing

1. Bake Yellow Cake as directed for muffin cups to make 24 cup-cakes. Make Creamy Vanilla Frosting; frost cupcakes.

2. Use desired candies for eyes and nose. Add candy coating wafers for ears. Sprinkle with nonpareil decors for hair. Pipe on mouth with decorating icing.

1 Cupcake (Cake and Frosting): Calories 300 (Calories from Fat 90); Total Fat 10g (Saturated Fat 5g; Trans Fat 0.5g); Cholesterol 50mg; Sodium 240mg; Total Carbohydrates 50g (Dietary Fiber 0g; Sugars 40g) • % Daily Value: Vitamin A 8%; Vitamin C 0%; Calcium 6%; Iron 4% • Exchanges: 1 Starch, 2 1/2 Other Carbohydrates, 2 Fat • Carbohydrate Choices: 3

Personalize It! Add hats to your clown cupcakes: Place sugar-style ice-cream cone, pointed end up, on top and edge of frosted cupcake. For eyes and eyebrows, attach candies with small amount of frosting to cone. Decorate remaining clown face and hat as desired.

Time-Saver Tip: Substitute 1 box (1 lb 2.25 oz) yellow cake mix with pudding for the Yellow Cake. Substitute 2 containers (1 lb each) vanilla creamy frosting for the Creamy Vanilla Frosting.

Frosted Cupcake Cones

1. Heat oven to 350°F. Make cake batter as directed on box, using water, oil and eggs. Fill each cone about half full of batter. Stand cones upright in regular-size muffin cups or 13 × 9-inch pan.

2. Bake 20 to 25 minutes or until toothpick carefully inserted in center comes out clean. Cool completely, about 1 hour.

3. Frost tops with frosting. For spiders, top cakes with miniature sandwich cookies and attach baking bits with small amount of frosting for eyes; insert pieces of string licorice into cookie filling for legs. For butterflies, insert pieces of shortbread cookies into frosting on cakes for wings; add pieces of string licorice for antennae. For snails, top cakes with round licorice candies and add baking bits for heads; add pieces of string licorice for antennae.

1 box (1 lb 2.25 oz) cake mix with pudding

Water, oil and eggs called for on cake mix box

30 to 36 flat-bottom ice-cream cones

1 container (12 oz) whipped frosting (any flavor)

Food colors, if desired

Miniature creme-filled chocolate sandwich cookies

Miniature candy-coated chocolate baking bits

Black and red string licorice

Fudge-striped shortbread cookies

Round licorice candies

1 Cone (Cone, Cake and Frosting): Calories 170 (Calories from Fat 60); Total Fat 7g (Saturated Fat 1.5g; Trans Fat 0g); Cholesterol 20mg; Sodium 135mg; Total Carbohydrates 24g (Dietary Fiber 0g; Sugars 15g) • **% Daily Value:** Vitamin A 0%; Vitamin C 0%; Calcium 4%; Iron 2% • **Exchanges:** 1½ Other Carbohydrates, 1½ Fat • **Carbohydrate Choices:** 1½

Easy Design Cupcakes

2 packages (3 oz each) cream cheese, softened

1/3 cup sugar

1 large egg

1 bag (6 oz) semisweet chocolate chips (1 cup)

1 box (1 lb 2.25 oz) devil's food cake mix with pudding

Water, oil and eggs called for on cake mix box

1 1/2 oz cream cheese (from 3-oz package), softened

4 teaspoons sugar

1. Heat oven to 350°F. Place paper baking cup in each of 24 regular-size muffin cups. In medium bowl, beat 2 packages cream cheese, 1/3 cup sugar and 1 egg with electric mixer on medium speed until smooth. Stir in chocolate chips; set aside.

2. Make cake mix as directed on box, using water, oil and eggs. Divide batter among cups. Top each with 1 tablespoon cream cheese mixture (mixture will sink into batter).

3. In small bowl, beat 1 1/2 ounces cream cheese and 4 teaspoons sugar with spoon until smooth. Spoon into corner of small plastic food-storage bag. Snip about 1/8 inch off corner of bag. Squeeze mixture onto batter in a small design to decorate tops of cupcakes.

4. Bake 20 to 25 minutes or until tops spring back when touched lightly. Cool 10 minutes; remove from pan to wire rack. Cool completely, about 50 minutes.

1 Cupcake (Cake and Frosting): Calories 220 (Calories from Fat 110); Total Fat 12g (Saturated Fat 5g; Trans Fat 0g); Cholesterol 45mg; Sodium 200mg; Total Carbohydrates 26g (Dietary Fiber 1g; Sugars 18g) • **% Daily Value:** Vitamin A 4%; Vitamin C 0%; Calcium 4%; Iron 8% • **Exchanges:** 1/2 Starch, 1 Other Carbohydrates, 2 1/2 Fat • **Carbohydrate Choices:** 2

Cupcake Pet Parade

1. Make White Cake as directed for 24 muffin cups to make cupcakes.

2. For cats, stir together ½ cup of the frosting and the chocolate syrup. Spread chocolate frosting over tops of 8 cupcakes. Cut small pieces of fruit snack for ears. Cut additional fruit snack into 1 × ¼–inch strips for whiskers. Use chocolate chips for nose and eyes. Arrange on frosting to make cat faces.

3. For rabbits, spread half of the remaining vanilla frosting over tops of 8 cupcakes. Flatten large white gumdrops with rolling pin; slightly fold and shape to form ears. Use pink gel to make inner ears. Cut fruit snack or flatten gumdrops and cut into 2 × ¼–inch strips for whiskers. Use baking bits for eyes and nose. Arrange on frosting to make rabbit faces.

4. For dogs, spread remaining vanilla frosting over tops of remaining 8 cupcakes. Break or cut cookies in half; press 2 halves in each frosted cupcake for ears. Use black gel for spots or streaks on face. Use pieces of gumdrops for eyes and nose. Flatten additional gumdrops for tongue. Arrange on frosting to make dog faces.

White Cake (page 143)

1 container (1 lb) vanilla creamy frosting

1 tablespoon chocolate-flavored syrup

Chewy fruit snack in 3-foot rolls, any flavor (from 4.5-oz box)

24 semisweet chocolate chips

16 large white gumdrops

1 tube (0.68 oz) pink decorating gel

24 miniature candy-coated chocolate baking bits

8 miniature creme-filled chocolate sandwich cookies

1 tube (0.68 oz) black decorating gel

Small gumdrops

1 Cupcake (Cake and Frosting): Calories 250 (Calories from Fat 100); Total Fat 11g (Saturated Fat 3.5g; Trans Fat 2.5g); Cholesterol 0mg; Sodium 240mg; Total Carbohydrates 35g (Dietary Fiber 0g; Sugars 26g) • **% Daily Value:** Vitamin A 0%; Vitamin C 0%; Calcium 6%; Iron 4% • **Exchanges:** 2½ Other Carbohydrates, 2 Fat • **Carbohydrate Choices:** 2

Ring-Around-the-Rosy Cupcakes

Baby Angel Food Cakes (page 136)

Creamy White Frosting (page 147)

Mini canapé cutters in circles or other shapes

Colored sugars in desired colors

1. Heat oven to 350°F. Bake and cool Baby Angel Food Cakes.

2. Make Creamy White Frosting. Frost cupcakes.

3. Gently press canapé cutter into frosting on cupcake where you want sugar design. Remove cutter and dip bottom edge into one of the sugars, then gently press cutter back into same stamped image on cupcake; remove. Continue with other cutters and colors of sugars.

1 Cupcake (Cake and Frosting): Calories 170 (Calories from Fat 30); Total Fat 3.5g (Saturated Fat 1g; Trans Fat 0.5g); Cholesterol 0mg; Sodium 40mg; Total Carbohydrates 32g (Dietary Fiber 0g; Sugars 28g) • **% Daily Value:** Vitamin A 0%; Vitamin C 0%; Calcium 0%; Iron 0% • **Exchanges:** 1 Starch, 1 Other Carbohydrates, 1/2 Fat • **Carbohydrate Choices:** 2

Personalize It! To add more color, bake these cute cupcakes in decorative baking cups found at cake decorating stores.

Time-Saver Tip: Substitute 1 box (1 lb) angel food cake mix for Baby Angel Food Cakes.

Flowerpot Cupcakes

Yellow Cake (page 144)

Scalloped paper baking cups

Creamy Vanilla Frosting (page 146)

Red liquid food color

24 new (clean) small clay flowerpots

1 bag (10.5 oz) pastel-colored miniature
   marshmallows

Flower-shaped candy lollipops,
   if desired

1. Bake Yellow Cake as directed for muffin cups to make 24 cupcakes, using scalloped paper baking cups. Make Creamy Vanilla Frosting; tint with 3 drops food color. Frost cupcakes.

2. Place scalloped paper baking cup in each flowerpot, pulling edge of liner over edge of pot. Place cupcakes in flowerpots. Top with mound of marshmallows to look like a chrysanthemum; add 1 marshmallow of different color in center.

1 Cupcake (Cake and Frosting): Calories 290 (Calories from Fat 120); Total Fat 13g (Saturated Fat 5g; Trans Fat 1.5g); Cholesterol 30mg; Sodium 200mg; Total Carbohydrates 40g (Dietary Fiber 2g; Sugars 29g) • **% Daily Value:** Vitamin A 4%; Vitamin C 0%; Calcium 0%; Iron 6% • **Exchanges:** 1 Starch, 1 1/2 Other Carbohydrates, 2 1/2 Fat • **Carbohydrate Choices:** 2 1/2

Personalize It! Planted Flower Cupcakes: Bake cupcakes as directed. Tint Creamy Vanilla Frosting (page 146) with desired food color; frost cupcakes. Sprinkle with candy sprinkles. Gently push flower-shaped candy lollipop into each cupcake. Place piece of green miniature marshmallow at base of lollipop for leaf.

Time-Saver Tip: Substitute 1 box (1 lb 2.25 oz) yellow cake mix with pudding for the Yellow Cake. Substitute 1 1/2 containers (1 lb each) vanilla creamy frosting for the Creamy Vanilla Frosting.

Design It! CANDY BUTTERFLIES

For each butterfly, cut a notch on straight sides of two candied fruit slices, slightly below center. Arrange slices for wings and notches for body as shown in diagram. Add string licorice for antennae.

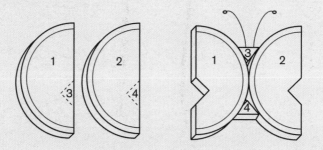

Bug Cupcakes

White Cake (page 143)

Creamy Vanilla Frosting (page 146)

Green, purple, blue or red paste or gel food color

Assorted candies (such as round mints, jelly beans, Jordan almonds, wafer candies, pieces from candy necklaces)

Miniature marshmallows

Colored sugar

String licorice

1 tube (4.25 oz) white decorating icing

1. Bake White Cake as directed for muffin cups to make 24 cupcakes. Make Creamy Vanilla Frosting. Tint frosting with desired food color; frost cupcakes.

2. Arrange candies on cupcakes to make bug heads, bodies and wings. In addition to candies, use whole marshmallows or sliced marshmallows sprinkled with colored sugar. Use pieces of licorice for antennae. For eyes, add dots of decorating icing.

1 Cupcake (Cake and Frosting): Calories 320 (Calories from Fat 100); Total Fat 11g (Saturated Fat 4g; Trans Fat 1.5g); Cholesterol 15mg; Sodium 220mg; Total Carbohydrates 51g (Dietary Fiber 0g; Sugars 41g) • **% Daily Value:** Vitamin A 4%; Vitamin C 0%; Calcium 6%; Iron 4% • **Exchanges:** 1/2 Starch, 3 Other Carbohydrates, 2 Fat • **Carbohydrate Choices:** 3 1/2

Time-Saver Tip: Substitute 1 box (1 lb 2.25 oz) white cake mix with pudding for the White Cake. Substitute 2 containers (1 lb each) vanilla creamy frosting for the Creamy Vanilla Frosting.

Graduation Cupcakes

1. Cut fruit snack rolls into 12-inch pieces. Cut each piece lengthwise into 4 strips, using knife and straightedge. Roll each strip in a spiral around handle of wooden spoon. Store at room temperature at least 8 hours to set curl.

2. Bake cake mix as directed on box for cupcakes, using water, oil and eggs. Cool completely, about 1 hour.

3. Tint half of frosting with food color. Frost cupcakes with frosting. Write "Congratulations" or "Congrats" and the graduate's name on cupcakes with decorating gel. Decorate other cupcakes with candy sprinkles and colored sugar. Unwrap fruit snack streamers from spoon handles. Reshape into desired curl; place on cupcakes. Cut additional fruit snack into small pieces and flower petal shapes; arrange on some of the cupcakes.

2 rolls chewy fruit snack in 3-foot rolls, any flavor (from 4.5-oz box)

1 box (1 lb 2.25 oz) cake mix with pudding

Water, oil and eggs called for on cake mix box

2 containers (12 oz each) fluffy white whipped frosting

Food color, if desired

Decorating gel (from 0.68-oz tube) in any color

Candy sprinkles, if desired

Colored sugar, if desired

Additional rolls of chewy fruit snack in 3-foot rolls, if desired

Miniature peanut butter cup candies, if desired

Chocolate-covered graham crackers, if desired

4. Top some of the cupcakes with candy graduation caps. To make, place small amount of frosting on bottom of peanut butter cup. Press graham cracker onto peanut butter cup. To make tassel, tightly roll up small square of chewy fruit snack; cut fringe in one end and press other end to center of graham cracker.

1 Cupcake (Cake and Frosting): Calories 250 (Calories from Fat 110); Total Fat 12g (Saturated Fat 3g; Trans Fat 0g); Cholesterol 25mg; Sodium 180mg; Total Carbohydrates 35g (Dietary Fiber 0g; Sugars 26g) • % Daily Value: Vitamin A 0%; Vitamin C 0%; Calcium 4%; Iron 2% • Exchanges: 2 1/2 Other Carbohydrates, 2 1/2 Fat • Carbohydrate Choices: 2

Personalize It! To celebrate a special anniversary, write "Happy Anniversary" on the cupcakes, and garnish with Sugared Roses (page 95).

Frog Cupcakes

White Cake (page 143)

Creamy Vanilla Frosting (page 146)

Green paste or gel food color

48 green miniature vanilla wafer
   cookies

48 red cinnamon candies

1 tube (4.25 oz) red decorating icing

Large red gumdrops

1. Bake White Cake as directed for muffin cups to make 24 cupcakes. Make Creamy Vanilla Frosting; reserve 2 tablespoons white frosting. Tint remaining frosting with food color to make green; frost cupcakes.

2. For ears, place 2 cookies near top edge of each cupcake, inserting on end so they stand up. Attach 1 cinnamon candy to each cookie with reserved white frosting. Add dots of white frosting for nostrils.

3. For mouth, pipe on red icing. Slice gumdrops; add slice to each cupcake for tongue.

1 Cupcake (Cake and Frosting): Calories 170 (Calories from Fat 50); Total Fat 6g (Saturated Fat 2.5g; Trans Fat 0g); Cholesterol 15mg; Sodium 50mg; Total Carbohydrates 30g (Dietary Fiber 0g; Sugars 28g) • **% Daily Value:** Vitamin A 4%; Vitamin C 0%; Calcium 0%; Iron 0% • **Exchanges:** 2 Other Carbohydrates, 1 Fat • **Carbohydrate Choices:** 2

Time-Saver Tip: Substitute 1 box (1 lb 2.25 oz) white cake mix with pudding for the White Cake. Substitute 2 containers (1 lb each) vanilla creamy frosting for the Creamy Vanilla Frosting.

Moon and Star Cupcakes

Yellow Cake (page 144)

Creamy White Frosting (page 147)

Blue paste or gel food color

White edible glitter, decorator sugar
crystals or candy sprinkles

Large yellow gumdrops

Large white gumdrops

1. Bake Yellow Cake as directed for muffin cups to make 24 cupcakes. Make Creamy White Frosting; tint with food color to make blue. Frost cupcakes. Sprinkle with edible glitter.

2. To make moons and stars, on piece of waxed paper, flatten gumdrops with rolling pin until $1\frac{7}{8}$ inches in diameter (sprinkle with sugar to keep from sticking). From yellow gumdrops, cut out crescent shapes with small sharp knife or small cookie cutter. From white gumdrops, cut out star shapes. Place on cupcake, inserting toothpick if needed to prop up.

1 Cupcake (Cake and Frosting): Calories 260 (Calories from Fat 100); Total Fat 11g (Saturated Fat 5g; Trans Fat 0g); Cholesterol 50mg; Sodium 240mg; Total Carbohydrates 38g (Dietary Fiber 0g; Sugars 28g) • **% Daily Value:** Vitamin A 8%; Vitamin C 0%; Calcium 6%; Iron 6% • **Exchanges:** 1 Starch, $1\frac{1}{2}$ Other Carbohydrates, 2 Fat • **Carbohydrate Choices:** $2\frac{1}{2}$

Personalize It! Add the Sun to your Moon and Star Cupcakes. Tint 2 containers (1 lb each) creamy white frosting with yellow food color; frost cupcakes. Decorate with candy corn to make outline of sun, and create a face with colorful candies.

Time-Saver Tip: Substitute 1 box (1 lb 2.25 oz) yellow cake mix with pudding for the Yellow Cake. Substitute 2 containers (1 lb each) white creamy frosting for the Creamy White Frosting.

Orange Soda Cake Cones

18 flat-bottom ice-cream cones

Orange Soda Cake (page 141)

1 container (1 lb) vanilla creamy frosting

¼ cup finely crushed orange-flavored hard candies

Additional finely crushed orange-flavored hard candies, if desired

9 striped candy sticks (5 inches long) or plastic straws

1. Heat oven to 350°F. Stand cones upright in regular-size muffin cups or 13 × 9–inch pan.

2. Make Orange Soda Cake as directed. Pour batter into cones, filling each to within about ¾ inch of top.

3. Bake 22 to 25 minutes or until toothpick inserted in center of cake comes out clean. Remove cones from muffin cups to wire rack. Cool completely, about 1 hour.

4. In small bowl, mix frosting and ¼ cup crushed candies. Spread over tops of cone cakes. Sprinkle with additional candies. Cut or break candy sticks in half; insert into each frosted cupcake cone.

1 Cone (Cone, Cake and Frosting): Calories 260 (Calories from Fat 90); Total Fat 11g (Saturated Fat 4.5g; Trans Fat 2g); Cholesterol 35mg; Sodium 230mg; Total Carbohydrates 39g (Dietary Fiber 0g; Sugars 25g) • **% Daily Value:** Vitamin A 4%; Vitamin C 0%; Calcium 2%; Iron 6% • **Exchanges:** 2½ Other Carbohydrates, 2½ Fat • **Carbohydrate Choices:** 2½

Cake Basics

Angel Food Cake

1½ cups powdered sugar

1 cup cake flour

1½ cups egg whites (about 12)

1½ teaspoons cream of tartar

1 cup granulated sugar

1½ teaspoons vanilla

½ teaspoon almond extract

¼ teaspoon salt

1. Move oven rack to lowest position. Heat oven to 375°F. In small bowl, mix powdered sugar and flour; set aside.

2. In large bowl, beat egg whites and cream of tartar with electric mixer on medium speed until foamy. Beat in granulated sugar, 2 tablespoons at a time, on high speed, adding vanilla, almond extract and salt with the last addition of sugar. Continue beating until stiff and glossy. Do not underbeat.

3. Sprinkle sugar-flour mixture, ¼ cup at a time, over meringue, folding in with rubber spatula just until sugar-flour mixture disappears. Push batter into ungreased 10 × 4–inch angel food (tube) cake pan. Cut gently through batter with metal spatula or knife to break air pockets.

4. Bake 30 to 35 minutes or until cracks in cake feel dry and top springs back when touched lightly. Immediately turn pan upside down onto heatproof funnel or bottle. Let hang about 2 hours or until cake is completely cool. Loosen side of cake with knife or long metal spatula; remove from pan.

1 Serving: Calories 180 (Calories from Fat 0); Total Fat 0g (Saturated Fat 0g; Trans Fat 0g); Cholesterol 0mg; Sodium 100mg; Total Carbohydrates 41g (Dietary Fiber 0g; Sugars 32g) • **% Daily Value:** Vitamin A 0%; Vitamin C 0%; Calcium 0%; Iron 4% • **Exchanges:** 1 Starch, 1½ Other Carbohydrates • **Carbohydrate Choices:** 3

BABY ANGEL FOOD CAKES: Divide batter evenly among 30 ungreased muffin cups (or line muffin cups with paper baking cups if desired). Bake 15 to 20 minutes or until cracks in cupcakes feel dry and tops spring back when touched lightly. Remove from pan to wire rack. Cool completely, about 30 minutes.

CHOCOLATE ANGEL FOOD CAKE: Substitute ¼ cup unsweetened baking cocoa for ¼ cup of the flour. Omit almond extract.

Applesauce Cake

1. Heat oven to 350°F. Grease bottom and sides of desired pan(s) with shortening; lightly flour.

2. In large bowl, beat all ingredients except raisins and walnuts with electric mixer on low speed 30 seconds, scraping bowl constantly. Beat on high speed 3 minutes, scraping bowl occasionally. Stir in raisins and walnuts. Pour batter into pan(s).

3. Bake as directed below or until toothpick inserted in center comes out clean. Cool 10 minutes; remove from pan(s) to wire rack. Cool completely, about 1 hour.

13 × 9−inch rectangle	45 to 50 minutes
two 8-inch rounds	40 to 45 minutes
two 9-inch rounds	40 to 45 minutes
one 9-inch round	40 to 45 minutes

1 Serving: Calories 280 (Calories from Fat 90); Total Fat 10g (Saturated Fat 2g; Trans Fat 1g); Cholesterol 30mg; Sodium 380mg; Total Carbohydrates 44g (Dietary Fiber 2g; Sugars 25g) • **% Daily Value:** Vitamin A 0%; Vitamin C 0%; Calcium 2%; Iron 8% • **Exchanges:** 1 Starch, 2 Other Carbohydrates, 2 Fat • **Carbohydrate Choices:** 3

2½ cups all-purpose flour or cake flour

1½ cups unsweetened applesauce

1¼ cups sugar

½ cup shortening

½ cup water

1½ teaspoons baking soda

1½ teaspoons salt

¾ teaspoon ground cinnamon

½ teaspoon ground cloves

½ teaspoon ground allspice

¼ teaspoon baking powder

2 large eggs

1 cup raisins

½ cup chopped walnuts

WHOLE WHEAT APPLESAUCE CAKE: Substitute 1¼ cups whole wheat flour for 1¼ cups of the all-purpose flour. Do not use cake flour.

Buttermilk Spice Cake

2 1/2 cups all-purpose flour or cake flour

1 cup granulated sugar

3/4 cup packed brown sugar

1/2 cup shortening

1 1/3 cups buttermilk

1 teaspoon baking powder

1 teaspoon baking soda

1 teaspoon salt

3/4 teaspoon ground cinnamon

3/4 teaspoon ground allspice

1/2 teaspoon ground cloves

1/2 teaspoon ground nutmeg

3 large eggs

1. Heat oven to 350°F. Grease bottom and sides of desired pan(s) with shortening; lightly flour.

2. In large bowl, beat all ingredients with electric mixer on medium speed 30 seconds, scraping bowl constantly. Beat on high speed 3 minutes, scraping bowl occasionally. Pour batter into pan(s).

3. Bake as directed below or until toothpick inserted in center comes out clean. Cool 10 minutes; remove from pan(s) to wire rack. Cool completely, about 1 hour.

13 × 9–inch rectangle	40 to 45 minutes
15 × 10 × 1–inch pan	30 to 35 minutes
two 8-inch rounds	40 to 45 minutes
two 9-inch rounds	35 to 40 minutes

1 Serving: Calories 260 (Calories from Fat 80); Total Fat 9g (Saturated Fat 2.5g; Trans Fat 1g); Cholesterol 45mg; Sodium 310mg; Total Carbohydrates 42g (Dietary Fiber 0g; Sugars 25g) • **% Daily Value:** Vitamin A 0%; Vitamin C 0%; Calcium 6%; Iron 8% • **Exchanges:** 1 Starch, 2 Other Carbohydrates, 1 1/2 Fat • **Carbohydrate Choices:** 3

Carrot Cake

1 1/2 cups sugar

1 cup vegetable oil

3 large eggs

2 cups all-purpose flour

1 1/2 teaspoons ground cinnamon

1 teaspoon baking soda

1 teaspoon vanilla

1/2 teaspoon salt

1/4 teaspoon ground nutmeg

3 cups shredded carrots (about 5 medium)

1 cup coarsely chopped nuts

1. Heat oven to 350°F. Grease bottom and sides of desired pan(s) with shortening; lightly flour.

2. In large bowl, beat sugar, oil and eggs with electric mixer on low speed about 30 seconds or until well blended. Add remaining ingredients except carrots and nuts; beat on low speed 1 minute. Stir in carrots and nuts. Pour batter into pan(s).

3. Bake as directed below or until toothpick inserted in center comes out clean. Cool 10 minutes; remove from pan(s) to wire rack. Cool completely, about 1 hour.

13 × 9–inch rectangle	40 to 45 minutes
two 8-inch rounds	30 to 35 minutes
two 9-inch rounds	30 to 35 minutes

1 Serving: Calories 350 (Calories from Fat 190); Total Fat 21g (Saturated Fat 3g; Trans Fat 0g); Cholesterol 40mg; Sodium 180mg; Total Carbohydrates 36g (Dietary Fiber 2g; Sugars 21g) • **% Daily Value:** Vitamin A 80%; Vitamin C 0%; Calcium 2%; Iron 8% • **Exchanges:** 1 1/2 Starch, 1 Other Carbohydrates, 4 Fat • **Carbohydrate Choices:** 2 1/2

APPLE CAKE: Substitute 3 cups chopped tart apples (about 3 medium) for the carrots.

Dark Cocoa Cake

1. Heat oven to 350°F. Grease bottom and sides of desired pan(s) with shortening; lightly flour. For cupcakes, place paper baking cup in each of 24 regular-size muffin cups.

2. In large bowl, beat all ingredients with electric mixer on low speed 30 seconds, scraping bowl constantly. Beat on high speed 3 minutes, scraping bowl occasionally. Pour batter into pan(s) or divide among muffin cups.

3. Bake as directed below or until toothpick inserted in center comes out clean. Cool 10 minutes; remove from pan(s) to wire rack. Cool completely, about 1 hour.

2¼ cups all-purpose flour

1⅔ cups sugar

¾ cup shortening

⅔ cup unsweetened baking cocoa

1¼ cups water

1¼ teaspoons baking soda

1 teaspoon salt

¼ teaspoon baking powder

1 teaspoon vanilla

2 large eggs

13 × 9–inch rectangle	40 to 45 minutes
two 8-inch rounds	30 to 35 minutes
two 9-inch rounds	30 to 35 minutes
two 8-inch squares	35 to 40 minutes
24 regular-size muffin cups	20 to 25 minutes

1 Serving: Calories 340 (Calories from Fat 130); Total Fat 15g (Saturated Fat 4g; Trans Fat 2g); Cholesterol 35mg; Sodium 350mg; Total Carbohydrates 48g (Dietary Fiber 2g; Sugars 28g) • **% Daily Value:** Vitamin A 0%; Vitamin C 0%; Calcium 2%; Iron 10% • **Exchanges:** 1 Starch, 2 Other Carbohydrates, 3 Fat • **Carbohydrate Choices:** 3

Double-Chocolate Cake

2 1/4 cups all-purpose flour

1 3/4 cups sugar

1/2 cup shortening

1 1/2 cups buttermilk

1 1/2 teaspoons baking soda

1 teaspoon salt

1 teaspoon vanilla

2 oz unsweetened baking chocolate, melted and cooled

2 large eggs

1 cup miniature chocolate chips

1. Heat oven to 350°F. Grease bottom and sides of desired pan(s) with shortening; lightly flour. For cupcakes, place paper baking cup in each of 24 regular-size muffin cups.

2. In large bowl, beat all ingredients except chocolate chips with electric mixer on medium speed 30 seconds, scraping bowl constantly. Beat on high speed 2 minutes, scraping bowl occasionally. Fold in chocolate chips. Pour batter into pan(s) or divide among muffin cups.

3. Bake as directed below or until toothpick inserted in center comes out clean. Cool 10 minutes; remove from pan(s) to wire rack. Cool completely, about 1 hour.

13 × 9–inch rectangle	40 to 45 minutes
two 9 × 5–inch loaves	35 to 40 minutes
two 8-inch rounds	40 to 45 minutes
two 9-inch rounds	35 to 40 minutes
two 9-inch squares	35 to 40 minutes
24 regular-size muffin cups	20 to 25 minutes

1 Serving: Calories 330 (Calories from Fat 120); Total Fat 14g (Saturated Fat 5g; Trans Fat 1g); Cholesterol 30mg; Sodium 310mg; Total Carbohydrates 47g (Dietary Fiber 2g; Sugars 31g) • **% Daily Value:** Vitamin A 0%; Vitamin C 0%; Calcium 4%; Iron 8% • **Exchanges:** 1 Starch, 2 Other Carbohydrates, 3 Fat • **Carbohydrate Choices:** 3

CHOCOLATE-CHERRY CAKE: Fold in 1/2 cup chopped maraschino cherries, well drained, with the chocolate chips.

Orange Soda Cake

1. Heat oven to 350°F. Grease bottom and sides of 9-inch square pan with shortening; lightly flour.

2. In medium bowl, beat all ingredients with electric mixer on low speed 30 seconds, scraping bowl occasionally. Beat on medium speed 2 minutes, scraping bowl occasionally. Pour batter into pan or divide among muffin cups.

3. Bake 33 to 37 minutes or until toothpick inserted in center comes out clean. Cool completely, about 1 hour.

2 cups all-purpose flour

3/4 cup sugar

1/3 cup butter or margarine, softened

1 cup orange-flavored soda pop

1 teaspoon baking powder

1/2 teaspoon baking soda

1/2 teaspoon salt

1/2 teaspoon grated orange peel

2 large eggs

1 Serving: Calories 260 (Calories from Fat 70); Total Fat 8g (Saturated Fat 4g; Trans Fat 0g); Cholesterol 65mg; Sodium 320mg; Total Carbohydrates 42g (Dietary Fiber 0g; Sugars 20g) • **% Daily Value:** Vitamin A 6%; Vitamin C 0%; Calcium 4%; Iron 8% • **Exchanges:** 1 Starch, 2 Other Carbohydrates, 1 1/2 Fat • **Carbohydrate Choices:** 3

Pound Cake

1. Heat oven to 300°F. Grease bottom and sides of desired pan(s) with shortening; lightly flour.

2. In large bowl, beat all ingredients with electric mixer on medium speed 30 seconds, scraping bowl constantly. Beat on high speed 2 minutes, scraping bowl occasionally. Pour batter into pan(s).

3. Bake as directed below or until toothpick inserted in center comes out clean. Cool 10 minutes; remove from pan(s) to wire rack. Cool completely, about 1 hour.

2 cups all-purpose flour

1 cup sugar

3 teaspoons baking powder

1/2 teaspoon salt

1/4 cup butter or margarine, softened

1/4 cup shortening

3/4 cup milk

1 teaspoon vanilla

2 large eggs

two 9 × 5–inch loaves	40 to 45 minutes
1 1/2-quart round casserole	65 to 75 minutes

1 Serving: Calories 180 (Calories from Fat 60); Total Fat 7g (Saturated Fat 2.5g; Trans Fat 0.5g); Cholesterol 35mg; Sodium 200mg; Total Carbohydrates 25g (Dietary Fiber 0g; Sugars 13g) • **% Daily Value:** Vitamin A 4%; Vitamin C 0%; Calcium 6%; Iron 6% • **Exchanges:** 1 Starch, 1/2 Other Carbohydrates, 1 1/2 Fat • **Carbohydrate Choices:** 1 1/2

Pumpkin-Gingerbread Cake

3¹/₂ cups all-purpose flour

2 cups sugar

1 cup butter or margarine, softened

1/2 cup light molasses

1/3 cup water

2 teaspoons baking soda

1 teaspoon salt

1 teaspoon ground cinnamon

1 teaspoon ground ginger

1/2 teaspoon baking powder

1/4 teaspoon ground nutmeg

1/4 teaspoon ground cloves

4 large eggs

1 can (15 oz) pumpkin (not pumpkin pie mix)

1. Heat oven to 350°F. Grease bottom and sides of desired pan(s) with shortening; lightly flour.

2. In large bowl, beat all ingredients with electric mixer on low speed 30 seconds, scraping bowl constantly. Beat on medium speed 3 minutes, scraping bowl occasionally. Pour batter into pan(s).

3. Bake as directed below or until toothpick inserted in center comes out clean. Cool 10 minutes; remove from pan(s) to wire rack. Cool completely, about 1 hour.

13 × 9–inch rectangle	**50 to 55 minutes**
two 1¹/₂-quart round casseroles	**60 to 75 minutes**

1 Serving: Calories 390 (Calories from Fat 130); Total Fat 14g (Saturated Fat 7g; Trans Fat 0.5g); Cholesterol 90mg; Sodium 450mg; Total Carbohydrates 60g (Dietary Fiber 2g; Sugars 34g) • **% Daily Value:** Vitamin A 100%; Vitamin C 0%; Calcium 6%; Iron 15% • **Exchanges:** 1 Starch, 3 Other Carbohydrates, 3 Fat • **Carbohydrate Choices:** 4

White Cake

1. Heat oven to 350°F. Grease bottom and sides of desired pan(s) with shortening; lightly flour. For cupcakes, place paper baking cup in each of 24 regular-size muffin cups or 36 mini muffin cups.

2. In large bowl, beat all ingredients except egg whites with electric mixer on low speed 30 seconds, scraping bowl constantly. Beat on high speed 2 minutes, scraping bowl occasionally. Beat in egg whites on high speed 2 minutes, scraping bowl occasionally. Pour batter into pan(s) or divide among muffin cups.

3. Bake as directed below or until toothpick inserted in center comes out clean or until cake springs back when touched lightly in center. Cool 10 minutes; remove from pan(s) to wire rack. Cool completely, about 1 hour.

2¼ **cups all-purpose flour**

1²/₃ **cups sugar**

²/₃ **cup shortening**

1¼ **cups milk**

3½ **teaspoons baking powder**

1 **teaspoon salt**

1 **teaspoon vanilla**

5 **egg whites**

13 × 9-inch rectangle	40 to 45 minutes
15 × 10 × 1-inch pan	25 to 30 minutes
two 8-inch rounds	23 to 28 minutes
two 9-inch rounds	30 to 35 minutes
24 regular-size muffin cups	20 to 25 minutes
36 mini (1¾ × 1-inch) muffin cups	10 to 15 minutes

1 Serving: Calories 320 (Calories from Fat 110); Total Fat 12g (Saturated Fat 3g; Trans Fat 2g); Cholesterol 0mg; Sodium 370mg; Total Carbohydrates 47g (Dietary Fiber 0g; Sugars 29g) • **% Daily Value:** Vitamin A 0%; Vitamin C 0%; Calcium 10%; Iron 8% • **Exchanges:** 1 Starch, 2 Other Carbohydrates, 2½ Fat • **Carbohydrate Choices:** 3

ALMOND CAKE: Substitute 1 teaspoon almond extract for the vanilla.

HAZELNUT CAKE: Add 1 cup ground hazelnuts (filberts) with ingredients.

MARBLE CAKE: Pour half of batter into another bowl. Mix 2 ounces unsweetened baking chocolate, melted and cooled, 1 tablespoon sugar, 2 tablespoons warm water and ¼ teaspoon baking soda. Stir into one batter. Spoon light and dark batters alternately into pan(s). Cut through batter several times for marbled design.

PASTEL MARBLE CAKE: Divide batter into 3 equal parts. Tint one part with 2 or 3 drops red food color and one part with 2 or 3 drops green food color; leave other part plain. Spoon batters alternately into pan(s).

Piece of Cake! If the recipe makes 24 cupcakes and you have only one 12-cup muffin pan, or if you want to make a three-layer cake and you have only two pans, cover and refrigerate the remaining batter while the first cupcakes or layers are baking.

Design It! TIC-TAC-TOE

Dip a piece of unwaxed dental floss or white sewing thread in liquid food color. Stretch it taut and press lines into frosted cake to make tic-tac-toe board. Make X's and O's with candies or cereals.

Yellow Cake

2¼ cups all-purpose flour

1½ cups sugar

½ cup butter or margarine, softened

1¼ cups milk

3½ teaspoons baking powder

1 teaspoon salt

1 teaspoon vanilla

3 large eggs

1. Heat oven to 350°F. Grease bottom and sides of desired pan(s) with shortening; lightly flour. For cupcakes, place paper baking cup in each of 24 regular-size muffin cups.

2. In large bowl, beat all ingredients with electric mixer on low speed 30 seconds, scraping bowl constantly. Beat on high speed 3 minutes, scraping bowl occasionally. Pour batter into pan(s) or divide among muffin cups.

3. Bake as directed below or until toothpick inserted in center comes out clean or until cake springs back when touched lightly in center. Cool 10 minutes; remove from pan(s) to wire rack. Cool completely, about 1 hour.

13 × 9–inch rectangle	35 to 40 minutes
two 8-inch rounds	30 to 35 minutes
two 9-inch rounds	25 to 30 minutes
two 8-inch squares	25 to 30 minutes
2-quart round casserole	65 to 75 minutes
24 regular-size muffin cups	20 to 25 minutes

1 Serving: Calories 290 (Calories from Fat 90); Total Fat 10g (Saturated Fat 4.5g; Trans Fat 0g); Cholesterol 75mg; Sodium 420mg; Total Carbohydrates 45g (Dietary Fiber 0g; Sugars 27g) • **% Daily Value:** Vitamin A 8%; Vitamin C 0%; Calcium 10%; Iron 8% • **Exchanges:** 1 Starch, 2 Other Carbohydrates, 2 Fat • **Carbohydrate Choices:** 3

ORANGE-COCONUT CAKE: Omit vanilla. Add 1 tablespoon grated orange peel and 1 cup flaked coconut with ingredients.

LEMON–POPPY SEED CAKE: Omit vanilla. Add 1 tablespoon grated lemon peel and 2 tablespoons poppy seed with ingredients.

Design It! PATCHWORK

Mark lines for cutting serving pieces in the frosting of a square or rectangular cake with a knife or toothpick. To make cake look like a patchwork quilt, fill the squares with chopped nuts, miniature candy-coated chocolate chips or candies, candy sprinkles, crushed candies, colored sugars, fruit-shaped candies, tinted coconut, chopped dried fruits, chocolate-dipped fruits, small shaped cookies or crackers or cereals.

Buttercream Frosting

In large bowl, beat powdered sugar, butter and shortening with electric mixer on low speed until blended. Beat in milk and vanilla on medium speed until smooth. If necessary, stir in milk, a few drops at a time, until spreadable. Frosts two 13 × 9–inch cakes, or fills and frosts two 8- or 9-inch two-layer cakes.

4 cups powdered sugar

1/2 cup butter or margarine, softened

1/2 cup shortening

2 to 3 tablespoons milk

1 teaspoon vanilla or almond extract

2 Tablespoons: Calories 150 (Calories from Fat 70); Total Fat 8g (Saturated Fat 3g; Trans Fat 1g); Cholesterol 10mg; Sodium 25mg; Total Carbohydrates 20g (Dietary Fiber 0g; Sugars 19g) • **% Daily Value:** Vitamin A 2%; Vitamin C 0%; Calcium 0%; Iron 0% • **Exchanges:** 1 1/2 Other Carbohydrates, 1 1/2 Fat • **Carbohydrate Choices:** 1

Chocolate Decorator Frosting

In 1-quart saucepan, melt chocolate and butter over low heat, stirring occasionally; remove from heat. Stir in powdered sugar and 1 tablespoon water. Beat with spoon until smooth. Beat in additional water, 1 teaspoon at a time, until spreadable.

1 oz unsweetened baking chocolate, chopped

1 teaspoon butter or margarine

1 cup powdered sugar

1 to 2 tablespoons boiling water

2 Tablespoons: Calories 90 (Calories from Fat 20); Total Fat 2.5g (Saturated Fat 1.5g; Trans Fat 0g); Cholesterol 0mg; Sodium 0mg; Total Carbohydrates 16g (Dietary Fiber 0g; Sugars 14g) • **% Daily Value:** Vitamin A 0%; Vitamin C 0%; Calcium 0%; Iron 0% • **Exchanges:** 1 Other Carbohydrates, 1/2 Fat • **Carbohydrate Choices:** 1

Creamy Chocolate Frosting

1/2 cup butter or margarine, softened

3 oz unsweetened baking chocolate, melted and cooled

3 cups powdered sugar

2 teaspoons vanilla

About 3 tablespoons milk

In large bowl, mix butter and chocolate with spoon or electric mixer on low speed. Beat in powdered sugar. Beat in vanilla and milk until smooth and spreadable. Frosts 13 × 9–inch cake, or fills and frosts an 8- or 9-inch two-layer cake.

2 Tablespoons: Calories 160 (Calories from Fat 70); Total Fat 8g (Saturated Fat 4g; Trans Fat 0g); Cholesterol 15mg; Sodium 35mg; Total Carbohydrates 21g (Dietary Fiber 0g; Sugars 19g) • **% Daily Value:** Vitamin A 4%; Vitamin C 0%; Calcium 0%; Iron 0% • **Exchanges:** 1 1/2 Other Carbohydrates, 1 1/2 Fat • **Carbohydrate Choices:** 1 1/2

CREAMY COCOA FROSTING: Substitute 1/2 cup unsweetened baking cocoa for the chocolate.

Creamy Vanilla Frosting

5 1/2 cups powdered sugar

2/3 cup butter or margarine, softened

2 teaspoons vanilla

About 3 tablespoons milk

In large bowl, beat powdered sugar and butter with spoon or electric mixer on low speed. Beat in vanilla and milk until smooth and spreadable. Frosts two 13 × 9–inch cakes, or fills and frosts two 8- or 9-inch two-layer cakes.

2 Tablespoons: Calories 160 (Calories from Fat 45); Total Fat 5g (Saturated Fat 2.5g; Trans Fat 0g); Cholesterol 15mg; Sodium 35mg; Total Carbohydrates 28g (Dietary Fiber 0g; Sugars 27g) • **% Daily Value:** Vitamin A 4%; Vitamin C 0%; Calcium 0%; Iron 0% • **Exchanges:** 2 Other Carbohydrates, 1 Fat • **Carbohydrate Choices:** 2

CREAMY ALMOND FROSTING: Substitute 1 1/2 teaspoons almond extract for the vanilla.

CREAMY CITRUS FROSTING: Omit vanilla. Substitute lemon or orange juice for the milk. Stir in 1/2 teaspoon grated lemon peel or 2 teaspoons grated orange peel.

PEANUT BUTTER FROSTING: Substitute peanut butter for the butter. Increase milk to 1/4 to 1/3 cup.

Design It! FEATHERS

- Dip a piece of unwaxed dental floss or white sewing thread in liquid food color. Stretch it taut and press lines into frosted cake, using new thread for each color. Immediately draw a knife back and forth across lines to make feather design.

- Or drizzle melted chocolate (from decorating bag or plastic bag with corner cut off) in lines about 1 inch apart across frosted or glazed cake. Immediately draw a knife back and forth across lines to make feather design.

Creamy White Frosting

In large bowl, beat powdered sugar and shortening with spoon or electric mixer on low speed. Beat in vanilla and milk until smooth and spreadable. Frosts two 13 × 9–inch cakes, or fills and frosts two 8- or 9-inch two-layer cakes.

4 cups powdered sugar

1/2 cup shortening

1/2 teaspoon clear vanilla or almond extract

2 to 3 tablespoons milk

2 Tablespoons: Calories 120 (Calories from Fat 40); Total Fat 4.5g (Saturated Fat 1g; Trans Fat 0.5g); Cholesterol 0mg; Sodium 0mg; Total Carbohydrates 20g (Dietary Fiber 0g; Sugars 19g) • **% Daily Value:** Vitamin A 0%; Vitamin C 0%; Calcium 0%; Iron 0% • **Exchanges:** 1 1/2 Other Carbohydrates, 1 Fat • **Carbohydrate Choices:** 1

Piece of Cake! Regular vanilla extract will work in this recipe, but clear vanilla will make for a whiter frosting. It is available at large supermarkets or specialty baking shops.

Design It! ABSTRACTS AND PLAIDS

Dip a piece of unwaxed dental floss or white sewing thread in liquid food color. Stretch it taut and press into frosted cake. Repeat, making desired abstract or plaid design. Use new thread for each color.

Cream Cheese Frosting

In large bowl, beat cream cheese, milk and vanilla with electric mixer on low speed until smooth. Gradually beat in powdered sugar, 1 cup at a time, until smooth and spreadable. Refrigerate any remaining frosted cake. Frosts 13 × 9–inch cake generously, or fills and frosts an 8- or 9-inch two-layer cake.

1 package (8 oz) cream cheese, softened

1 tablespoon milk

1 teaspoon vanilla

4 cups powdered sugar

2 Tablespoons: Calories 140 (Calories from Fat 35); Total Fat 4g (Saturated Fat 2.5g; Trans Fat 0g); Cholesterol 15mg; Sodium 35mg; Total Carbohydrates 24g (Dietary Fiber 0g; Sugars 23g) • **% Daily Value:** Vitamin A 4%; Vitamin C 0%; Calcium 0%; Iron 0% • **Exchanges:** 1 1/2 Other Carbohydrates, 1 Fat • **Carbohydrate Choices:** 1 1/2

Caramel Frosting

1/2 cup butter or margarine

1 cup packed brown sugar

1/4 cup milk

2 cups powdered sugar

1. In 2-quart saucepan, melt butter over medium heat. Stir in brown sugar. Heat to boiling, stirring constantly; reduce heat to low. Boil and stir 2 minutes. Stir in milk. Heat to boiling; remove from heat. Cool to lukewarm, about 30 minutes.

2. Gradually stir in powdered sugar. Place saucepan of frosting in bowl of cold water. Beat with spoon until smooth and spreadable. If frosting becomes too stiff, stir in additional milk, 1 teaspoon at a time, or heat over low heat, stirring constantly. Frosts 13 × 9–inch cake, or fills and frosts an 8- or 9-inch two-layer cake.

2 Tablespoons: Calories 170 (Calories from Fat 50); Total Fat 6g (Saturated Fat 3g; Trans Fat 0g); Cholesterol 15mg; Sodium 45mg; Total Carbohydrates 29g (Dietary Fiber 0g; Sugars 28g) • **% Daily Value:** Vitamin A 4%; Vitamin C 0%; Calcium 0%; Iron 0% • **Exchanges:** 2 Other Carbohydrates, 1 Fat • **Carbohydrate Choices:** 2

White Decorator Frosting

6 1/4 cups powdered sugar

3/4 cup shortening

3/4 teaspoon clear vanilla or almond extract

1/2 cup milk

In large bowl, beat powdered sugar and shortening with spoon or electric mixer on low speed. Beat in vanilla and milk until smooth. If necessary, stir in additional milk, a few drops at a time, until smooth and spreadable.

2 Tablespoons: Calories 140 (Calories from Fat 45); Total Fat 5g (Saturated Fat 1g; Trans Fat 1g); Cholesterol 0mg; Sodium 0mg; Total Carbohydrates 24g (Dietary Fiber 0g; Sugars 23g) • **% Daily Value:** Vitamin A 0%; Vitamin C 0%; Calcium 0%; Iron 0% • **Exchanges:** 1 1/2 Other Carbohydrates, 1 Fat • **Carbohydrate Choices:** 1 1/2

White Mountain Frosting

2 egg whites

1/2 cup sugar

1/4 cup light corn syrup

2 tablespoons water

1 teaspoon vanilla

1. In medium bowl, beat egg whites with electric mixer on high speed just until stiff peaks form; set aside.

2. In 1-quart saucepan, stir sugar, corn syrup and water until well mixed. Cover and heat to rolling boil over medium heat. Uncover and boil 4 to 8 minutes, without stirring, to 242°F on candy thermometer or until small amount of mixture dropped into cup of very cold water forms a firm ball that holds its shape until pressed. For an accurate temperature reading, tilt the saucepan slightly so mixture is deep enough for thermometer.

3. Pour hot syrup very slowly in thin stream into egg whites, beating constantly on medium speed. Add vanilla. Beat on high speed about 10 minutes or until stiff peaks form. Frosts 13 × 9–inch cake, or fills and frosts an 8- or 9-inch two-layer cake.

2 Tablespoons: Calories 30 (Calories from Fat 0); Total Fat 0g (Saturated Fat 0g; Trans Fat 0g); Cholesterol 0mg; Sodium 10mg; Total Carbohydrates 7g (Dietary Fiber 0g; Sugars 5g) • **% Daily Value:** Vitamin A 0%; Vitamin C 0%; Calcium 0%; Iron 0% • **Exchanges:** 1/2 Other Carbohydrates • **Carbohydrate Choices:** 1/2

Piece of Cake! To get an accurate temperature reading on the thermometer, it may be necessary to tilt the saucepan slightly. It takes 4 to 8 minutes for the syrup to reach 242°F. Preparing this type of frosting on a humid day may require a longer beating time.

FLUFFY BROWN SUGAR FROSTING: Substitute packed brown sugar for the granulated sugar and decrease vanilla to 1/2 teaspoon.

FLUFFY COCOA FROSTING: Sift 1/4 cup unsweetened baking cocoa over frosting and fold in until blended.

Chocolate Glaze

ABOUT 1 CUP GLAZE

1 bag (6 oz) semisweet chocolate chips (1 cup)

1/4 cup butter or margarine

2 tablespoons light corn syrup

In 1-quart saucepan, heat all ingredients over low heat, stirring constantly, until chocolate chips are melted and mixture is smooth and thin enough to drizzle. Cool slightly. Glazes 13 × 9–inch cake, 10-inch angel food cake or tops of two 8- or 9-inch layer cakes.

1 Tablespoon: Calories 90 (Calories from Fat 50); Total Fat 6g (Saturated Fat 3.5g; Trans Fat 0g); Cholesterol 10mg; Sodium 25mg; Total Carbohydrates 9g (Dietary Fiber 0g; Sugars 7g) • **% Daily Value:** Vitamin A 2%; Vitamin C 0%; Calcium 0%; Iron 0% • **Exchanges:** 1/2 Other Carbohydrates, 1 Fat • **Carbohydrate Choices:** 1/2

White Chocolate Glaze

ABOUT 1/2 CUP GLAZE

1/2 cup white vanilla baking chips

2 tablespoons light corn syrup

1 1/2 teaspoons water

In 1-quart saucepan, heat all ingredients over low heat, stirring constantly, until chips are melted and mixture is smooth and thin enough to drizzle. Cool slightly. Glazes top of an 8- or 9-inch layer cake.

1 Tablespoon: Calories 110 (Calories from Fat 50); Total Fat 5g (Saturated Fat 3g; Trans Fat 0g); Cholesterol 0mg; Sodium 20mg; Total Carbohydrates 14g (Dietary Fiber 0g; Sugars 12g) • **% Daily Value:** Vitamin A 0%; Vitamin C 0%; Calcium 4%; Iron 0% • **Exchanges:** 1 Other Carbohydrates, 1 Fat • **Carbohydrate Choices:** 1

Petits Fours Glaze

ABOUT 3 CUPS GLAZE

1 bag (2 lb) powdered sugar

1/2 cup water

1/2 cup light corn syrup

2 teaspoons almond extract

1 to 3 teaspoons hot water

In 3-quart saucepan, stir all ingredients except hot water. Heat over low heat, stirring frequently, until sugar is dissolved; remove from heat. Stir in hot water, 1 teaspoon at a time, until glaze is pourable.

1 Tablespoon: Calories 90 (Calories from Fat 0); Total Fat 0g (Saturated Fat 0g; Trans Fat 0g); Cholesterol 0mg; Sodium 0mg; Total Carbohydrates 21g (Dietary Fiber 0g; Sugars 20g) • **% Daily Value:** Vitamin A 0%; Vitamin C 0%; Calcium 0%; Iron 0% • **Exchanges:** 1 1/2 Other Carbohydrates • **Carbohydrate Choices:** 1 1/2

Helpful Nutrition and Cooking Information

Nutrition Guidelines

We provide nutrition information for each recipe that includes calories, fat, cholesterol, sodium, carbohydrates, fiber and sugars. Individual food choices can be based on this information.

Recommended intake for a daily diet of 2,000 calories as set by the Food and Drug Administration

Total Fat	Less than 65g
Saturated Fat	Less than 20g
Cholesterol	Less than 300mg
Sodium	Less than 2,400mg
Total Carbohydrates	300g
Dietary Fiber	25g

CRITERIA USED FOR CALCULATING NUTRITION INFORMATION

- The first ingredient was used wherever a choice is given (such as 1/3 cup sour cream or plain yogurt).
- The first ingredient amount was used wherever a range is given (such as 3- to 3 1/2-pound cut-up broiler-fryer chicken).
- The first serving number was used wherever a range is given (such as 4 to 6 servings).
- "If desired" ingredients and recipe variations were not included (such as sprinkle with brown sugar, if desired).
- Only the amount of a marinade or frying oil that is estimated to be absorbed by the food during preparation or cooking was calculated.

INGREDIENTS USED IN RECIPE TESTING AND NUTRITION CALCULATIONS

- Ingredients used for testing represent those that the majority of consumers use in their homes: large eggs, 2% milk, 80%-lean ground beef, canned ready-to-use chicken broth and vegetable oil spread containing not less than 65 percent fat.
- Fat-free, low-fat or low-sodium products were not used, unless otherwise indicated.
- Solid vegetable shortening (not butter, margarine, nonstick cooking sprays or vegetable oil spread as they can cause sticking problems) was used to grease pans, unless otherwise indicated.

EQUIPMENT USED IN RECIPE TESTING

We use equipment for testing that the majority of consumers use in their homes. If a specific piece of equipment (such as a wire whisk) is necessary for recipe success, it is listed in the recipe.

- Cookware and bakeware without nonstick coatings were used, unless otherwise indicated.
- No dark-colored, black or insulated bakeware was used.
- When a pan is specified in a recipe, a metal pan was used; a baking dish or pie plate means ovenproof glass was used.
- An electric hand mixer was used for mixing only when mixer speeds are specified in the recipe directions. When a mixer speed is not given, a spoon or fork was used.

COOKING TERMS GLOSSARY

BEAT: Mix ingredients vigorously with spoon, fork, wire whisk, hand beater or electric mixer until smooth and uniform.

BOIL: Heat liquid until bubbles rise continuously and break on the surface and steam is given off. For rolling boil, the bubbles form rapidly.

CHOP: Cut into coarse or fine irregular pieces with a knife, food chopper, blender or food processor.

CUBE: Cut into squares 1/2 inch or larger.

DICE: Cut into squares smaller than 1/2 inch.

GRATE: Cut into tiny particles using small rough holes of grater (citrus peel or chocolate).

GREASE: Rub the inside surface of a pan with shortening, using pastry brush, piece of waxed paper or paper towel, to prevent food from sticking during baking (as for some casseroles).

JULIENNE: Cut into thin, matchstick-like strips, using knife or food processor (vegetables, fruits, meats).

MIX: Combine ingredients in any way that distributes them evenly.

SAUTÉ: Cook foods in hot oil or margarine over medium-high heat with frequent tossing and turning motion.

SHRED: Cut into long thin pieces by rubbing food across the holes of a shredder, as for cheese, or by using a knife to slice very thinly, as for cabbage.

SIMMER: Cook in liquid just below the boiling point on top of the stove; usually after reducing heat from a boil. Bubbles will rise slowly and break just below the surface.

STIR: Mix ingredients until uniform consistency. Stir once in a while for stirring occasionally, often for stirring frequently and continuously for stirring constantly.

TOSS: Tumble ingredients (such as green salad) lightly with a lifting motion, usually to coat evenly or mix with another food.

METRIC CONVERSION GUIDE

Volume

U.S. Units	Canadian Metric	Australian Metric
¼ teaspoon	1 mL	1 ml
½ teaspoon	2 mL	2 ml
1 teaspoon	5 mL	5 ml
1 tablespoon	15 mL	20 ml
¼ cup	50 mL	60 ml
⅓ cup	75 mL	80 ml
½ cup	125 mL	125 ml
⅔ cup	150 mL	170 ml
¾ cup	175 mL	190 ml
1 cup	250 mL	250 ml
1 quart	1 liter	1 liter
1½ quarts	1.5 liters	1.5 liters
2 quarts	2 liters	2 liters
2½ quarts	2.5 liters	2.5 liters
3 quarts	3 liters	3 liters
4 quarts	4 liters	4 liters

Weight

U.S. Units	Canadian Metric	Australian Metric
1 ounce	30 grams	30 grams
2 ounces	55 grams	60 grams
3 ounces	85 grams	90 grams
4 ounces (¼ pound)	115 grams	125 grams
8 ounces (½ pound)	225 grams	225 grams
16 ounces (1 pound)	455 grams	500 grams
1 pound	455 grams	½ kilogram

Measurements

Inches	Centimeters
1	2.5
2	5.0
3	7.5
4	10.0
5	12.5
6	15.0
7	17.5
8	20.5
9	23.0
10	25.5
11	28.0
12	30.5
13	33.0

Temperatures

Fahrenheit	Celsius
32°	0°
212°	100°
250°	120°
275°	140°
300°	150°
325°	160°
350°	180°
375°	190°
400°	200°
425°	220°
450°	230°
475°	240°
500°	260°

NOTE: The recipes in this cookbook have not been developed or tested using metric measures. When converting recipes to metric, some variations in quality may be noted.

Index